MIDGARD

MIDGARD

JEANNE HULL GODFROY

NEW DEGREE PRESS

MIDGARD

ISBN 979-8-88504-560-5 *Paperback*

979-8-88504-886-6 *Kindle Ebook*

979-8-88504-677-0 *Ebook*

To my friend, Alexia Wellons, and to Mike Temple, Mel Shields, Diane Bauer, Frank Boyd, Dan Fitzgerald, Nancy Rue, and Janet and Fred Toti—the teachers who always saw other paths for me that I could not see for myself.

CONTENTS

AUTHOR'S NOTE

When I was in the second grade, my teacher told me there was a hole in the sky. I was too young to comprehend what an ozone layer was or how hairspray and refrigerators had caused the hole in the first place. The only thing I understood was that, if the hole was not fixed, my family and I would be unable to live outside for the rest of our lives, and I was terrified of that prospect. Thankfully, humankind intervened to heal the wound its efforts to modernize had created, and I returned to my normal childhood.

I grew up an avid reader who enjoyed learning about history, science, and the world far more through stories than from facts in textbooks, but I lost touch with that aspect of myself as I left my childhood behind. After I finished high school, I attended West Point and joined the US Army. I saw the remnants of a bloody civil war in Bosnia, witnessed a second war in Iraq, studied international relations and civil war for my doctorate, and taught those topics to future military officers. And then I married, left the Army, and became a mother in just over three years—major transition points that rocked my world.

Amidst a subsequent identity crisis, I tried academia, the policy realm, the tech community, and consulting, but none of those career paths felt like the right fit. Then the universe intervened to help me out. During an icebreaker exercise at a certification course in 2019, I blurted out, "I am a closeted novelist." That statement came from some unacknowledged creative reservoir inside, and it rang true as nothing else had. The only problem was that I needed to come up with a story to write.

Fortunately (or, perhaps, providentially!) the idea for *Midgard* came fast on the heels of that startling recognition. I had recently read Yvon Chouinard's *Let My People Go Surfing*, which renewed my interest in humans' adverse impact on the planet. It also illustrated another principle that resonated with me—stewardship of the abundant, but not limitless, resources of our amazing Earth. I delved further into the topic by reading, watching, and listening to other books, films, and lectures about humans' impact on their habitat. In the process, it occurred to me that my son was likely to grow up in a much harsher and less hospitable world than I did if humanity failed to act. Scientists, world leaders, and wonks alike made similar assertions, but it seemed they were unwilling or unable to come to a consensus and act. So, I thought—and hoped—others like me might prefer science fiction to scientific journals and might decide to do their own homework on environmental degradation if primed by a good story. Therein lies the foundation for *Midgard*.

This book is designed for people who care about the world and their role in it. I hope you enjoy reading the story as much as I enjoyed putting it together. Then perhaps you, too, will look more closely at your own talents and consider how you might best serve the interests of humankind and its fellow creatures on Earth.

PART I

Don't grieve. Anything you lose comes around in another form.

—RUMI

CHAPTER ONE:

THE TUNNEL

June 2154

"All right, Richmond. This is your last chance. Are you ready?"

Yes, asshole, I'm ready for all of this to be over so I never have to deal with you again.

Aloud, Sam said, "I'm ready, sir." His voice shook as he stared into the three-foot-wide hole in the wall in front of him and wished he was anywhere else in the world. He rested his clammy hands on the oiled knees of his slicker suit as he crouched, preparing to spring forward into the black opening.

"Very well," the proctor continued, "I'll start the countdown. Ten, nine, eight..."

Sam barely heard the numbers as he strove to control his breathing. *Ten minutes or less and this will be over for good, one way or another.* A vision of reading his Accessions results, getting the position of his dreams, and receiving congratulatory messages from his mother and classmates crossed his mind in the seconds before the hard reality of his present situation hit home.

"...three, two, one, go!"

A horn sounded, and spectators cheered as Sam dove into the entrance of the dreaded "Tunnel." It consisted of one hundred meters of interconnected tubes, openings, and ladders he had to navigate in total darkness. The horizontal cylinders gradually decreased in diameter until they funneled to a gap so narrow a person had only just enough room to wriggle through. As if the course itself were not challenging enough, it also had a time constraint. Candidates had only five minutes to make it from one end to the other. Most of the Tunnel's hopefuls failed at least once or twice before achieving success or giving up. Sam was on his fifth—and final—attempt, and the stakes could not have been higher.

After five years of advanced academic and technical instruction, Sam and his peers at the academies of higher education had entered several months' worth of preparation for the all-important employment Accessions process. Once per year, eligible adults had the opportunity to apply or "bid" for available employment opportunities. The most desirable positions required candidates to complete a grueling assessment regimen that would ultimately determine the trajectory of their lives.

For the majority of candidates, the allure of top-level jobs was the fact that they came with the best rations, housing, and licensing opportunities among other benefits. But Sam knew all of those things were superficial distractions for the general public, most of whom were unaware of how dire the situation on Earth was. Unlike them, he knew only a handful of elite positions were worth competing for because they alone could ensure him a reasonable lifespan. Anything short of those opportunities was a death sentence for anyone in his peer group or, at least, those who planned to live into their middle years.

Sam also understood that he was more fortunate than most. He had access to one of the academies through his mother, Dr. Miranda Richmond, who served in one of those supercritical positions. The instruction he received at the

Verdi Academy enhanced his considerable intellectual talents, and he had also taken full advantage of its exclusive Accessions' preparative courses. But even those extensive programs had been insufficient to get him through the dreaded Tunnel.

The Tunnel—known officially as the Restricted Movement Test—was the final obstacle in the way of his ambitions. The ostensible purpose of the Tunnel was to test for claustrophobia, but its true purpose, as Sam had discovered after each successive failure, was about overcoming one's worst fears and the panic that came with them.

Sam pushed those thoughts to the back of his consciousness as he hurled himself out of the first stretch of cylinders, grabbed the ladder, and cursed as he slipped and banged his chin on one of its rungs. He shook off the pain, eased himself down three or four steps, and felt against the wall with one hand to find the entrance to the next tube.

When he felt nothing but wall, his heart skipped a beat. *They must have changed the course.* The thought ignited panic, and the sound of his racing heartbeat pounded in his ears. He forced himself to focus. *Find the hole. Find the hole. Find the hole*, he repeated to himself as he continued down. Finally, he felt a gap at the top of one of his feet, dropped to the bottom of the ladder, and heaved himself into the next hole. This tube was considerably smaller, and as he slunk forward, it felt like a giant hand that squeezed him progressively tighter as he continued forward.

The first month of Sam's Accessions testing had gone far better than he had hoped. He excelled at the academic and skills-based exams, had passed his physical with flying colors, for which he privately thanked his mother, and made it through the ever-ambiguous psychological testing with no major aberrations. In addition, and with considerable practice and plenty of bruises, scrapes, and minor sprains, he had managed to pass all of the obstacle courses. Fortunately, the combatives tests were pro forma for the positions Sam wanted. He was miserable at hand-to-hand fighting and abhorred physical contact with any human being outside of those he was closest to. Thanks to his overall performance, however, he was among the most competitive candidates for the opportunities he sought, with one glaring exception.

And I'm into the final stretch. Sam clamored up the next ladder into a hole that was slightly larger than shoulder width. At this stage of the Tunnel, all he could hear was his own jagged breathing and, once again, he took a few seconds to get it under control. Like a worm he had once watched during a class on soil regeneration, he wriggled his way through the first half of the shaft and felt the all-too-familiar icy feeling in his extremities as the chute steadily shrank around him.

It was pitch black, empty, and isolating. Alone with his breath, Sam felt isolated and terrified. And then the faint sounds of the crowd reminded Sam that life lay beyond this all-important, smothering impediment.

"Come on, Sam! Come on!"

"Geez. You're almost there, man. You can do this!"

"You're gonna make it this time! Just keep moving forward!"

The shouts of encouragement sounded as if they came from a great distance, though Sam knew he was within ten feet of them. Grunting with discomfort, he inched further into the narrowing crevasse and suffered the crushing pressure of concrete and stone.

It's all in your head, Sam. Claustrophobia is, by definition, an irrational fear. You can, therefore, rationalize yourself out of it. This mantra—the one Sam had created for himself to get through this ordeal—felt hollow now that he was back in the fray. He reminded himself that he was now closer to the end than he had ever been before and, in a bizarre moment of clarity, likened the experience to going through the birth canal. If he could survive, a new life awaited him on the other side.

Too bad none of us can remember being born. This unwanted thought reignited the panic he worked so hard to repress.

"One minute, forty seconds remaining, Richmond, and then we're pulling you out of there."

The proctor's taunting voice penetrated Sam's unnerved psyche and lit the fuse he needed to propel himself through the underground labyrinth's final section. He knew it was physically possible for his oiled body to slither through the narrowest point of the course, but he struggled to translate that thought into decisive action.

He clenched his jaw and laid his head flat to one side, gripped as tightly as his slimy fingers permitted, and launched himself forward with his toes. Bile rose up in the back of his throat as the tapered canal further smushed his body. But he forced himself to repeat the maneuver and inched toward the noise.

Just a little bit farther. Sam moved into the last section of the shaft and, as he tried to move forward, felt that his head was stuck. He reached out his trembling, aching arms and attempted to maneuver his cranium toward them to no avail. Dizzy and faint, he thought he might asphyxiate.

"You're sooo close, Sam! I can see your hair," a woman's voice screamed with excitement that bordered on alarm. Sam would have recognized that voice anywhere. It was his neighbor, childhood playmate, and best friend, Tamara Ashraf. They had tested together for most of the Accessions process, as they were interested in similar opportunities. She had struggled in many of the tests, but even she had made it through the Tunnel. For a split second, he pictured her in his mind and saw her large brown eyes widen with the joyful glow he knew would await him once he succeeded.

I can reach her. Sam pressed his cheek further into the bottom of the shaft and found that his head was no longer stuck. He advanced and increased his velocity as he maneuvered toward the sound of her voice.

An eternity passed. On his next shift forward, Sam felt noticeably cooler air at his fingertips along with—*Yes!*—the Tunnel's edge. He slid to get a better grip and heard the proctor count out the remaining seconds:

"...five, four, three..." The count was lost in the roaring in Sam's ears and the shouts of the crowd as he slid up and out of the dark passageway and into the light.

CHAPTER TWO:

THE LOCKER ROOM

Sam's relief at successfully navigating the Tunnel was temporarily eclipsed by his body's reaction to the experience. Two test monitors hauled him out of the crack and helped him up. They dashed out of the way as he heaved, crouched over, and expelled the contents of his stomach. The spectators' cheers turned to cries of amused disgust before a member of the medical staff rushed over to assist him. She gave him a bowl and terse instructions to keep his head over it while she checked him over.

"Congratulations, Richmond. You actually passed the Restricted Movement Exam. I guess fifth time's a charm."

"Thanks," Sam gasped. *You sadistic Tier IV bastard.* By coincidence or design, Sam had had the same test proctor—who went by the moniker Marquis—for each of his Tunnel attempts. Marquis took obvious pleasure in his job, especially with struggling candidates. He had ribbed Sam mercilessly about each botched attempt, called him every variation of "coward" or "loser," and frequently mentioned that Sam would be lucky to get into any tier at all given his demonstrated ineptitude. But Sam knew better than to bait the proctor's sadism with anything but a neutral response.

Marquis was unable to hide his disappointment. "I will post your results within the hour. You have the rest of the week to complete your Accessions application before bidding closes."

"Yes, sir," Sam managed before returning his attention to the bowl. Marquis grunted, whether in delight or revulsion Sam neither knew nor cared. He closed his eyes and let the medical staffer fuss over him while his nausea abated. When he opened them, he sought Tamara's slight figure in the stands and spotted her mop of unruly black curls—ringlets that bounced with the enthusiasm of their owner—easily. She beamed at him, her dimples as deep in her cheeks as he had ever seen them as she mouthed the words, "Are you okay?" He gave her a tired smile and nodded while the staffer took his vitals.

Satisfied, she handed Sam a dissolvable pill with gruff instructions to take it immediately. He complied and sputtered within seconds. It had a sharp, spicy flavor with a bitter edge that made his mouth feel like it was full of flaming thistles. He glanced over at the other two candidates farther down the bench; their red faces and watering eyes suggested a similar reaction. After a minute or so, his limbs ceased shaking, the nausea dissipated, and he felt a burst of energy shoot through his extremities.

"Okay, folks," the medical assistant announced with an upbeat trill. "You are cleared to depart the testing area. Please make your way out through the locker room and leave those slicker suits in the textile recycling hamper. Make sure that you contact me if you feel poorly tonight or tomorrow. My information is preloaded in your EAMS devices."

Sam heard one of his colleagues smother a groan as he followed him into the locker room. There, he stripped, dumped the slicker suit in the hamper, and stepped under the spritzer in the first empty stall he found. He stifled a cry as the water hit the latest set of abrasions the Tunnel had inflicted.

Alarmed, the young man in the adjacent stall called out to him. "Are you okay, Sam?"

"I'm fine, thanks. Just a little banged up."

"Okay, just checking. I thought you might pass out or—or something."

Over the noise of the spritzers, Sam heard a choked sob. *This is awkward.* "You had a good run, Peyton." *Which is true,* Sam said to himself, *if you count making it out of the Tunnel but over time as a "good run."*

Peyton turned off the water and stepped into one of the standing dryers, brushing his cheeks. "Not good enough, though."

Sam paused and let the water run over his face while he considered an appropriate response. Clearly, one was required. "You could still try again before the end of the week. There's time—"

"No, Sam, I don't have it in me to go through that... that farce of an assessment again. Honestly, I don't know how you had the guts to do it more than twice. Although—" he studied Sam's dripping figure, "you can cram yourself into small spaces more easily than I can." Peyton gestured to his long, lean limbs that towered over Sam.

Sam's reply was automatic. "Oh, well, one's size does not really matter for the Tunnel. They calibrate the shaft width based on height and weight for each entrant."

Peyton pressed his lips together and turned away, grabbing a towel as he went. "Geez. You really know how to cheer a guy up, Sam."

"I'm sorry. It was not my intention to—"

"To what? Highlight my incompetence? Rub in the fact that I'm probably going to get stuck as a Tier III now, Tier II if I'm lucky? No, I didn't think that was your intention." Peyton shook his head and stalked out of the dryer with an aura of angry defeat.

Sam looked after him, slack-jawed, his planned strategic assurances unspoken.

Peyton had his back turned when Sam entered the changing area. He was fixated on the newscast displayed on the far wall. Sam hitched up his towel and moved closer so he could hear what the reporter said.

"...and today we mark another somber milestone. Two days ago, Alan Martinez of the Tahoe Transformation Initiative failed to show up for work. He was formally declared missing this morning. There are no signs of foul play, and police believe he has likely joined the ranks of the Disappeared, making him the one-hundredth missing person from the region this year. Anyone with information about Alan's whereabouts should immediately contact their municipal or interior police representative at..."

Another one. And he was a Tier III. The unexplained disappearances had begun over three years ago. At least that was when the information had first been reported in the public domain. At first, the government did not seem to notice or care about the sudden surge in missing persons. When the numbers steadily increased, however, national leaders became concerned. They created task forces and initiated a country-wide effort to determine where their citizens—especially their most talented ones—had gone. But no one had been able to find a single clue as to their whereabouts.

Last year, he and Tamara had lost their favorite teacher to the Disappeared, and a Tier I scientist who worked with

Miranda Richmond had disappeared four months ago. That loss had caused a furor of activity given the man's renown. At that point, Miranda informed Sam that the numbers of those missing were far higher than the government was willing to admit.

The newscast finished, and Peyton noticed Sam standing behind him. He glared at Sam, anger and hostility written all over his face, but Sam considered how he would feel if their roles were reversed and held his peace. He turned to the locker area to find his clothes when an unfamiliar young man came over to him holding out a crisp beige utility suit.

"Hey, man," he said to Sam, "I think this uniform is yours. It is way too small for me or—" he looked at Peyton's gangly frame, "that gentleman over there."

"Thanks," Sam responded before taking the suit and pointing to its attached label. "It also has my initials on it."

"Oh, right." The young man blushed. "I should have seen that." He grabbed the remaining uniform from the bench and checked the label. "Yup. H.R. instead of S.R. My mistake." He squeezed himself into the trousers and stood up. Sam observed a tall, muscular body that made even Peyton look underdeveloped. A ripping sound echoed off the locker room's walls when H.R. put his left arm into the suit's upper half, and he smirked when he discovered a hole in one of the armpits. "Oh, well. We won't be wearing these much longer."

"True. But I appreciate you not trying to put this one on," Sam commented, noting how baggy his own suit felt as he slid his legs into the trousers. At twenty-two, Sam knew that five feet seven inches was all the height his genes would ever grant him, but his reedy thinness made him appear even shorter. Although all Academy students received superior rationing packets than their peers, Sam's slight build made him look as if he was constantly malnourished. He was, however, deceptively wiry and tough, if uncoordinated, and far less fragile than he appeared.

H.R. chuckled. "Look on the bright side. At least you didn't have to squeeze this body through that last part of the Tunnel."

Peyton's snort of derision echoed off of the tiled walls as he left. "Ramirez"—or so the lettering on his back left pocket suggested—turned toward the noise and knit his brows again. "I didn't realize that was some kind of joke." He smiled at his unintentional blunder, revealing teeth that gleamed strong and white against golden-brown skin.

Sam was momentarily struck by the warmth and good humor that emanated from the other young man. "It isn't," he responded as he fished under the bench for his shoes and socks.

"Oh. Well, I'm Hector, by the way. I don't think we've crossed paths before."

"I'm pleased to meet you," Sam responded stiffly. "I'm Sam, and I'm from Verdi. You're from the Sparks Academy down south."

"How did you—"

Sam pointed to Hector's naked right shoulder. "Whatever outfit you were wearing this morning left quite an impression. Can you please pass me those boots?"

Ramirez glanced down at a faded red "SA" encircled by a ring of shapes that looked as if they had once been stars. "Nice call, bud," he said as he grabbed and tossed a set of boots to his target with the graceful, fluid motion of a practiced athlete. Sam, who was unprepared for the speed or accuracy of the throw, threw up his hands to defend himself, which sent the boots flying into the wall behind him.

"Sorry! I should have made sure you were looking." Before Sam could recover, Hector leaped over the bench and swooped up the boots with the same nimble efficiency, ripping his trouser leg in the process. He glanced at Sam's chest. "Richmond, eh? Hey, wait a second. Are you the Sam Richmond who is on top of the national examination leaderboard?"

Sam blushed as he took the boots. He was uncomfortable with the praise but pleased. "Yes, I am although I am at the very bottom of this particular list," he responded and gestured to the door that led out to the Tunnel's egress.

"Hey, don't be so hard on yourself. A pass is a pass after all, especially when it comes to this thing. I thought I heard the proctor say this was like your tenth time or something like that. That's impressive."

Sam scrutinized Hector's features for mockery but saw nothing but admiration on his face and relaxed. "It was my fifth timed trial, actually, though I also had several practice runs in between. I wouldn't have taken the Tunnel test at all if it wasn't absolutely necessary for—for the things I am interested in doing." He hurriedly changed the subject. "Finishing the Tunnel on your first attempt is also quite an accomplishment."

"Yeah, I guess so," Hector responded. "I purposely saved it for last because I heard so many horror stories about it. I thought that leaving it until the end would make me force myself to finish." He shrugged. "I actually thought it was kind of fun, though it's not the type of fun I would volunteer myself for again."

Sam experienced an internal shudder. "You are the only person I've met who would ever call that experience fun. But you look like a guy who is going for one of those Tier

I physical endurance positions. The Mars program if I had to guess."

Hector grinned again. "Yeah, I guess it's pretty obvious what I'm good at. Do I have Mars tattooed on my forehead or something? No, bud, I didn't mean literally," he joked when he saw the direction of Sam's gaze.

Sam fiddled with the fasteners on his boots to hide his reddening face. "It's the most difficult option, and you seem to enjoy challenges."

"Don't we all? If we didn't, we wouldn't be here." He looked Sam up and down. You look like a prospective meteorologist to me."

"Well, looks can be deceiving." The words left his mouth before he could hold them back, and he glanced at Hector to see if he had offended him too.

Instead, Hector laughed. "It's okay, Sam. You don't have to tell me your plans if you don't want to. Believe it or not, I respect discretion, and I'm sure you have your reasons." He held out an unassuming, flat gray cuff to Sam. "By the way, I'm pretty sure this one is yours. I checked this time, and it has your initials on it." The metal band dangled from his fingertips, looking like a toy in his overly large hands. "That nurse out there really threw me when she called it the EAMS. I thought they were just called wristlets."

"It stands for Enhanced Activity Management System—E-A-M-S." He found himself giving Hector one of his own rare smiles as he placed the device on his wrist. Normally it took him several interactions to warm to people, but Hector's warmth and humor drew him like a magnet.

"You have a good memory, too," Hector commented as he donned his own. "But I prefer the name wristlet. It sounds less intimidating."

"It has been my experience that calling something by its true name has the effect of making it less intimidating. And having a good memory is an asset in some circumstances while a detriment in others." Sam looked meaningfully back toward the testing area.

Hector frowned as he absorbed Sam's pronouncements. "Both are excellent points," he agreed and examined Sam as if he had just discovered a blooming flower on a cactus.

Then Sam noticed that Hector's eyes were a startling bluish-green—much lighter than his dark complexion would have suggested. "Thanks. It was nice meeting you," he called as Hector walked toward the door.

"Same here. And good luck with your bid submission. I think you would make an intriguing colleague, Sam Richmond. I hope our paths cross again."

Sam bent over to lace up his boots. "That circumstance is unlikely given that we're not bidding on the same programs." The tone was harsher than he intended. The pill's effects had started to wear off, and Sam suddenly realized how utterly exhausted he was after the months of stressful trials. He stood up to apologize, but Hector was gone, and Sam found himself alone with the reverberations of his empty words.

CHAPTER THREE:

THE OPTIONS

The A-framed entryway to the university's genetics complex stood in stark contrast to the bulbous cluster of buildings it guarded. A shadow overhead partially obscured the blistering sun, and to the east, a cluster of graphite-colored cumulonimbus clouds piled over the scorched mountains. Sam felt the vibrations of the tempest's growls and hurried inside.

As he removed his protective suit—a necessity that day given the heat and air quality—he remembered how frightened he had been of storms as a child. Once, he had asked his mother why the sun did not fight or run away from abusive winds, smoke, and storms; it was strange to him that the sun suffered such cruelty with resignation. Instead of giving him the scientific answer, however, Miranda had told him a story about how the sun won a competition with the wind by the use of persuasion rather than brute force.

If only we lived in a world like that, he mused, as he approached the security desk to his mother's building. Andrea, the guard, recognized him immediately and waved him forward.

"Hello, Sam! Good to see you and congrats on passing the Tunnel! I'll let Dr. Richmond know you've arrived."

Does the whole world know about that already? He shook his head as he realized that Tamara had probably broadcast the news far and wide by now. "Thank you," he said with as much grace as he could muster. "I won't be long. I know she's busy."

"Yes," Andrea agreed, "She sure puts in long hours. You know," she continued, "she's one of my heroes." She cocked her head to one side and smiled. "You've got some large shoes to fill."

He flushed with the effort involved in not snapping at yet another person that afternoon. This was about the thousandth time he had heard that comment in his lifetime, and unless he made a name for himself, he would have to listen to it in perpetuity. "Very true," he agreed tersely. "Which is why I prefer not to advertise my shortcomings."

Now it was her turn to blush. "I didn't mean—I get that, I suppose. I just hope my daughter has half as many options as you when her bidding window opens." She checked the facility terminal to hide her discomfiture. "It looks like you're cleared to proceed to the office. Congrats again," she finished with an awkward wave toward the genetics department.

The thick steel doors slid open, and Sam walked past the robot sentinels to a hallway full of office suites. Digital images of the faculty glared down at him as if he had already failed something else. When he reached a portrait of a young woman with black hair, slate-blue eyes, and a serious expression, he stopped and read its caption.

Dr. Miranda Richmond
Distinguished Selectee, Class of 2125
Assessed: Human Resiliency Program
Current Position: Assistant Director,
Human Engineering Project

"Human Resiliency Program," he whispered with a combination of longing and apprehension.

"HRP," as it was more commonly known, was the umbrella term for worldwide efforts to create artificial habitats to house civilization if—or, rather when—the Earth's environment finally collapsed. Sam's mother was a senior leader for The Human Engineering Project, which fell underneath the HRP's portfolio. Its eponymous purpose was to enhance the genetic capacity of humans so they could survive the diseases and privations of a less permissive future.

Miranda Richmond was a star pioneer in the field. She made a name for herself when she developed a successful treatment for a prehistoric bacterium that was released from melting Antarctic glaciers. Her efforts had prevented a global outbreak and saved innumerable lives, and now she worked to spread that knowledge far and wide.

Whenever Sam thought about his mother's considerable legacy, he felt a mix of pride in her achievements and doubt that he could ever hope to live up to them. When he had expressed those thoughts aloud to her, however, she had sat him down and explained the futility of the comparison. "You and I are different, Sam, and judgment only serves the interests of our weaknesses at the expense of our strengths. Remember that each time you compete with someone else."

With that memory in mind, he walked into her office. The woman behind the desk was a grayer, more lined version of the picture in the hallway, but her face had the same angular beauty and intensity. Her eyes, which lit up at her son's arrival, were shadowed with fatigue and a world-weariness that had been absent in her younger self.

Miranda stood up to greet her son. "What wonderful news about the Tunnel, Sam. I am so proud of you. How do you feel?" She motioned for him to sit down as the door closed behind him.

He blew out his breath and pushed his own dark hair off of his forehead. "I'm not really sure yet, Mom. Relieved, I guess, but I expect that feeling will not last long."

She nodded in sympathy as she sat across from him. "No," she agreed, "but everything will be settled in the next week or so regardless."

She took a moment to memorize his appearance, knowing she would see very little of him in the years to come. One of the side effects of the genetic enhancements that had helped his generation survive was an increasing number and type of asymmetrical features. Drooping eyelids, crooked noses, and odd-sized digits were common. Sam had one ear and one eye that were significantly higher than their counterparts, and his mouth—like his mother's—was warped into a shape that gave him a constant, unintentional smirk. But his skin, though sallow, was clear, and his hazel eyes were expressive and intelligent, which helped to balance out his otherwise awkward appearance.

Sam interpreted her taut posture as anxiety on his behalf. "The Tunnel proctor said my results will post by tomorrow, so I made my interview appointment for tomorrow afternoon. That still gives the Accessions Committee almost a week to finalize primary and waitlist opportunities. Aside from the Tunnel and some of my combatives scores, I'm still one of the most competitive candidates for Human Engineering."

Miranda pressed her lips together. "I wish you had waited until we had spoken before setting the interview."

He was taken aback. "What do you mean? We've discussed my interview strategy for months. Now that the Tunnel is over, I can—unless..." He felt the blood drain out of his face. "Unless all of those positions are filled. I must have waited too long then." The last words came out in the flat, final tones of someone who had heard—but did not yet fully accept—grave news.

She shook her head vigorously. "No, Samuel, that isn't it at all. There are still plenty of slots, at least as far as I know. At any rate, you know I removed myself from selection proceedings this year because of your bid, so I'm not tracking the openings as closely as I normally would."

For the second time that day, Sam felt relief close on the heels of tension, and he covered his face with his hands. "What is it then?"

She fidgeted in her chair. "It's good news actually," she said, and he looked up at her expectantly. "You see, Sam, I've been nominated to lead the Human Engineering Project." She smiled as she spoke, but her eyes were veiled.

Sam struggled to take in the news. "That is—well, unexpected." Heat replaced the chill that surged through him just moments before, and he added, "Wow. I mean—well, Mom, that is incredible news." A rare exultant smile spread over his face on her behalf as much as his own. Then he knit his brows together. "Aren't you being promoted way earlier than we—I mean you—planned?"

"The timing could have been better," she agreed, "but perhaps it's for the best."

"I don't understand," he said, and his frown deepened.

She sighed, stood up, and walked around her office, absently glancing at the posted accolades. "I didn't expect the promotion for a few more years, but circumstances being what they are..." She trailed off, recalled herself, and then faced Sam.

"I see," he said slowly. "The government wants you to accelerate the progress you've made, but they also need someone with your cachet to give everyone renewed hope."

"Yes, exactly," she said and looked around as if an unwanted audience were listening. "Oh, and incidentally, the news about my promotion is close hold until the formal announcement. Please keep it to yourself for now."

Sam was about to ask whether her office was under surveillance, but she shook her head. "I'm just being paranoid. We've discussed this but..."

"I know. Time is running out. Our work last summer proved as much." They had developed some models together based on the most accurate climate data they could piece together along with information accessible to only select groups of scientists. Regardless of how they adjusted their algorithms, they came up with one common conclusion: Civilization had less than fifty years remaining before the Earth would rid itself of its most parasitic species.

Sam sat back in his chair, closed his eyes, and steeled himself. "How long before the end comes?"

She stopped pacing and took the chair next to him. "Our last data says we have about twenty years left. Thirty at most." She watched his hazel eyes turn black as his pupils dilated, and he looked away. She was tempted to put her hand on his shoulder to steady him, but she knew the gesture was more likely to disturb him instead.

With a shaky breath, he said, "But I still don't understand how this—I mean our—situation affects my Accessions plans. If anything, it means I'll be working for you regardless of which Human Engineering position I am offered, if," he cautioned, "I am offered one at all. I know I'm interviewing late, but as you said, some positions are likely still available, and I know I can help you."

"I know you can, too, honey, perhaps more than you realize." She paused. "Have you considered the Capsule Project as an alternative to Human Engineering?"

"What? Where did that idea...?" He trailed off as his brain tried to process this startling directive. The Capsule Project was the most promising of the Human Resiliency habitats. As its name suggested, it consisted of hundreds of enclosed domes on the Earth's surface, each capable of hosting clusters of five hundred to a thousand people. And some rumors said the North American effort intended to expand more quickly than planned. But Sam hated the thought of living in enclosed environments and thus had not seen Capsule as a great option, his Tunnel success notwithstanding.

Miranda's voice intruded on those reservations. "Think about it. Capsule is the farthest along of the Human Resiliency efforts and—"

"The best Human Engineers will be given the opportunity to live in a Capsule environment," he finished. To himself, he added, *When the government is forced to make these choices in a decade or so.*

She smiled. "I knew you would catch on. Also, I could use your eyes and ears to make sure my team's efforts are maximized."

That, too, makes sense, he thought. Aloud, he asked, "Who in Capsule is standing in the way of your progress?"

Miranda chewed on her lower lip. "Officially, no one is holding us back. The Capsule leadership has been the most supportive of our efforts of any program. But—" Here she lowered her voice. "I would, of course, leave it to you to find and clear any obstacles in our path."

"Yes," Sam replied absently while his mind raced. "I understand. I'll consider it. What you propose is a good strategy, but I need to get used to the idea, and quickly since my interview is tomorrow."

"I know, honey. And I trust you will find your own way to improve upon my suggestion." She narrowed her eyes when she saw him open his mouth to say something and then close it. "What is it, Sam?"

The words burst out of him from some deep reservoir of doubt. "What about Tam?"

Miranda was taken aback. She raised her eyebrows. "What about her?"

Sam took a deep breath. "I—I can't leave her behind to die."

Miranda suddenly looked as old as she felt, but her resolve got the better of her, and her expression hardened. "As you know, Tamara is eligible to interview for Capsule although her chances are not nearly as promising as yours." When Sam opened his mouth to protest, she gestured for him to remain silent. "You underestimate her abilities. She has tremendous value apart from her genetic advantages, and she may yet exceed even her own expectations."

Sam was skeptical. "You might be right, but I would feel better if you could provide some assistance behind the scenes."

"I see." She blew out the air in her lungs and stared into the distance to think. "Yes," she said after a moment, "I do have a few strings I could pull but—" she looked hard at Sam, "it must be her choice."

Sam smiled for the first time that day. "I think I can plant the idea, but I might need your help to encourage its growth."

"I'll see what I can do, but I can't promise anything." Miranda thought for a moment. "Actually, I saved a little surprise for you and Tamara. Why don't you invite her over to dinner before her interview? We can celebrate together for one last time before you embark on your new lives."

"A surprise?" Sam raised an eyebrow. He was not sure he could take too many more of them today.

Miranda chuckled. "Not like the Capsule idea, Sam. You'll love this one. I promise. Anyhow," she sighed as she returned to her desk, "I have a bunch of work to wrap up before I can leave today, so I'll be late again as usual. And I believe you have a new interview strategy to develop." She gave him a half-smile and turned back toward the terminal at her desk.

"Yes," he said seriously, "I do. I guess I'll see you at home." He stood up and moved toward the door.

"Have a safe trip back." She watched him exit through her eyelashes and wiped away the tears she had held back during their conversation. "And I love you, Sam," she whispered, as the door shut him from view.

CHAPTER FOUR:

THE INTERVIEW

The waiting area at the interview center was empty save for Sam and a young woman dressed in the taupe of one of the vocational schools. She looked around at the empty seats and nervously tapped her foot on the floor.

"Are we the only ones here?" she asked.

"Apparently." He tried to smile.

The black-paneled door opposite the entryway opened and a man in the yellow uniform of the Accessions Committee entered carrying a tablet. "Richmond, Samuel James," he called as he zeroed in on Sam. "Welcome. I am Mark Watson, your interview mediator. Please follow me."

Sam stood and moved briskly to still the tremors in his legs as Watson led him into a dark room. He pointed to a low chair in the room's center, gestured for Sam to be seated, and proceeded to read a prepared script from his tablet.

"Samuel J. Richmond. Welcome to your Accessions interview. Your position requests have been reviewed by the prospective employers to whom you submitted your file. Those who expressed interest were invited to participate in your interview today. As you may already be aware, you are not authorized to disclose the contents of this discussion." He paused and made eye contact with Sam. "Do you have any questions at this time?"

"No, sir." Sam's voice was even, but his heart pounded in his ears so loudly it was difficult for him to hear.

"Good," Watson said with a smile that was meant to be reassuring but appeared to Sam as a grimace. "We will begin in approximately five minutes." He departed, his shoes clicking a sound that beat in time with Sam's pulse.

Breathe. Focus. Every calming technique Sam had ever learned involved those two words, and he clung to them now. After his heart rate slowed sufficiently, he took in his surroundings. Discussing the interviews was a taboo topic, reinforced by law, and curiosity soon overtook his nerves.

The Accessions Committee, he mused, had selected an appropriately intimidating aesthetic. The black, semi-circular table that faced him looked like it had grown out of the floor like a tumor. A large chair at its center was marked, *Mediator.* The other positions were chair-less and were numbered from one to ten in Roman numerals with the even numbers to the left and the odd numbers on the right. The space between the mediator's chair and the number "I" was larger than the rest of the evenly spaced positions, and it marred the symmetry of the arrangement.

Sam frowned. The place markers made sense, but the spacing puzzled him. He was confident the Roman numerals represented the employment categories known as tiers. Due to the scarcity of jobs—and the intense competition surrounding them—the government had centralized the process of matching eligible applicants to job opportunities. Occupations were organized into tiers based on how vital their associated industry was to the country's preservation. Food and water rations, housing, and other benefits were tied to each tier, and the more valued positions in the upper tiers came with the best of everything; the scraps went to everyone else.

Watson returned and seated himself at the table. "Your panelists will arrive shortly." He put his palm on an object at his seat, and a soft chime sounded. Two three-dimensional human holograms emerged behind the places marked "I" and "II." A few seconds later, a third person's image appeared in the "IV" position. The digital images greeted one another and engaged in some banter as Sam realized what the open space was for.

He sickened with disappointment and fear. It was reserved for the Human Resiliency Program representative. And it was empty.

The HRP positions were so critical to survival that they were in their own exclusive category outside of the Tiering system. Typically, less than fifty spots were available in each Accessions window, and they had obviously been finalized before Sam managed to finish his testing.

And, thanks to his mother, Sam was one of the few who knew that program was the only real option for anyone who planned to survive the next quarter-century.

Fortunately, his brain functioned well on autopilot, and he was able to answer the Tier I, II, and IV questions with a level voice that masked his inner turmoil. *This is what an out-of-body experience feels like,* he thought irreverently, as his mechanical answers delighted his inquisitors.

His trance was interrupted by a strange blip of static in the empty spot near Watson. The Tier II delegate stopped in the middle of his sentence and gaped in astonishment as the hologram of a tall, wiry figure with close-cropped silver hair emerged. Sam's heart leapt.

"Apologies for my tardiness," the late arrival said. "I had an emergency to attend to. Please proceed." He gave his colleagues a magnanimous wave and then stared at Sam with a look so piercing he almost forgot a hologram and not a human form stood in the room.

Sam recognized the imposing figure from the training pamphlets, videos, simulations, and advertisements he had studied for years. Here, in his Accessions interview, was Dr. Stephan Gage, head of the Capsule Project and deputy director of the entire Human Resiliency Program, one of the most powerful men in the country and, quite possibly, the world.

Dr. Gage waited politely for the Tier II representative to stutter his way through the remainder of his questions, which Sam answered half-heartedly. He was still starstruck by Dr. Gage's appearance.

Finally, Watson turned the table over to Dr. Gage, who nodded and smiled at Sam. "Mr. Richmond," he began, "it is a pleasure to meet you. You're a bit late to this game, though."

"Yes, sir," Sam managed to eke out.

"There is no need for you to be concerned, Mr. Richmond. In fact, circumstances seemed to have worked in your favor. I had résumé fatigue and stepped away from the review process for a time. Yours showed up as a last-minute qualifier and caught my attention." He considered Sam for a moment. "Your packet was exceptional, in most respects, that is."

Sam felt his internal temperature rise and color his cheeks. "I see how it might be advantageous, sir, but the last-minute submission was not intentional."

"I did not think it was," Gage agreed, "but I appreciate your honesty." He turned to Watson and the others. "Ms. Cortland, gentlemen, please excuse us for a few moments. I have some sensitive questions I'd like to ask this young man based on what I unearthed in his file, and they're better suited for a private conversation."

"Of course, Dr. Gage," Watson said, eager to please. The others voiced their assent, and their holograms disappeared one by one. Watson made some obsequious gestures and backed out of the room as if Gage were royalty instead of a project administrator.

Gage's eyes trailed Watson, and he smirked before returning to Sam, who was still in shock.

Gage was the first to break the staring contest, as he looked down to check his notes. "I see you did some interesting modeling last summer with human genetics." He looked up and folded his hands under his chin. "Why did you prefer my program over Human Engineering?"

Sam felt naked in front of this man. "It was a difficult decision," Sam admitted. "I considered many factors, including—" He stopped himself. Given Gage's earlier statement, he knew only total candor would suffice, and he shook his head to negate his previous comments.

Gage raised his eyebrows, but Sam exhaled hard and pressed on. "Truthfully, sir, I don't know. I was drawn to Capsule from the time I first learned about the project, but I needed my mo—I mean I, well, I suppose I needed permission to give myself that option." He wondered if Gage could see him blushing through the hologram's interface.

Gage seemed satisfied, if not approving, of the answer. "I guessed as much and, as you have likely deduced, I know whose permission you needed. Now, tell me why I should select you for Capsule."

Don't overthink it. Miranda's parting advice that morning echoed in Sam's awareness. He raised his eyes until they were level with Dr. Gage's. "Because you need someone who thinks like I do and knows what I know on your team."

"Oh? Please continue," Dr. Gage prompted with a smile of amusement.

This is it, Sam thought as the words spilled out of him. "Because I know we have less than thirty years to make Capsule a success before the end comes."

Gage raised an eyebrow but kept his smile. "So, young man, you predict an apocalypse soon then?"

"Not exactly, sir." He gave himself space to steady his voice. In the last century, the world had witnessed wars, nuclear events, natural disasters, pandemics, and even a near-miss with space debris that threatened to destroy all life on the planet. But no single event precipitated humankind's current predicament.

"I believe the available models we have on the planet's sustainability are incorrect," Sam continued. "Specifically, they underestimate the combined damage to the environment from overconsumption, pollution, and erosion, and they don't accurately account for genetic attrition. Additionally, most of the arable and habitable land on the planet is receding at an exponential rate because of shifting weather and climate patterns. If my calculations are correct, the Earth will soon be unable to host any but the most resilient life forms. Separately, these issues create minor catastrophes, but when combined, they will prove far more damaging than any fiery Armageddon."

Gage's smile had gradually disappeared as Sam spoke, and his brow now furrowed in consternation. "How confident are you in that assessment?"

Sam did not hesitate. "Completely."

A shadowy figure leaned in toward Gage's left ear, giving his digital image a Janus-like face—one side light, and the other side shaded. Gage held a consultation in low tones with the other person—or persons. Sam could not read lips well enough to determine the contents of the discussion, but he saw Dr. Gage nod slowly before the dark form stepped out of his image.

He looked at Sam, who struggled to conceal his shaking limbs. Seconds passed in total silence that felt like forever.

"Impressive," Gage said at last. "Impressive, but risky to say such things outside of this room or—" he caught himself, "with other trusted agents."

"I know that, sir," Sam responded. "I know this knowledge, if widely known, would create instability that would harm any efforts to save our species. Therefore, I tend to keep those thoughts to myself." Calm settled over Sam as the words left his lips. It felt good to speak the truth to someone besides Miranda. The feeling was exquisite but fleeting.

"Hmmm. That remains to be seen." Gage seemed to ponder Sam's response for a moment and then his hologram abruptly transitioned from a seated to standing posture.

"Good luck to you, Mr. Richmond." He signaled to an unseen entity before he disappeared, leaving behind a brief glow on the periphery of where his image had been.

Sam sat stunned, alone, and in the dark with no more certainty about his future than when he finished the Tunnel.

CHAPTER FIVE:

THE FRUIT

A deluge hit the valley on Sam's return journey from the interview, and his wristlet buzzed with flash flood and mudslide warnings. He stayed alert as he departed the e-train platform. It was not a long walk, but the pathways had become a swampy mush that made travel precarious, especially when burdened with a protective suit. By the time he made it to the small, reinforced fiberglass bungalow he shared with his mother, he was covered in mud.

Ten minutes in the decontamination chamber soon rectified the worst of the mess, and Sam entered the main living area clean if bedraggled. He saw Tamara and Miranda seated across from one another at the galley island, both doubled over with laughter.

A splash of color caught his eye, and he made a sound of pleasurable surprise. Both women looked up, and Tamara wiped tears from her eyes as she beamed at him.

Miranda stood up. "Well, honey, it looks like the interview got the best of you instead of the other way around," she jested. But her eyes glinted intensely as they scanned her son.

"Hey, Sam! Look what your mom brought home!"

Tamara's exclamation was superfluous as Sam gawked at the lavish feast, the likes of which he had not seen in years. The island was littered with small plates and bowls of fruit—real, fresh fruit not the dehydrated, supplement-infused husks that normally passed for such fare. Bright red strawberries, green and pink-cheeked apples, purplish blueberries, and sliced cucumbers dulled the galley's faded green recycled glass tiles into insignificance.

"Don't worry. It isn't contraband," Miranda said with a wry smile as she gestured him over. "I've been saving my special rations for a while, and today was a good opportunity to cash them in."

"Thanks, Mom," Sam responded hoarsely. He joined Tamara at the island, and his stomach growled as the vibrant colors swam before him. "You were right. This is an excellent surprise."

"I told you it would be." She piled some apple slices and berries onto a plate and held it out to him. "Enjoy."

"Well, don't just stare at it. Dig in!" Tamara chided while Sam sat, mesmerized.

Miranda chuckled. "He's always been selective about his food, even in the absence of such choice." She bit into an apple but continued to observe him closely for signs of how his interview went.

Tamara wrinkled her nose. "I'd just call him picky."

"You're both right," Sam interjected. He looked at his mother to acknowledge the unasked question. "Although I remain open to suggestion."

"Try a strawberry. They're my favorite." Tamara leaned toward him and playfully snatched one of the berries off his plate. She tilted her head back and dropped it into her mouth. "Mmmmmm. This is amazing." She turned back toward Sam and smirked at him coyly. "Sam, you are missing out."

He pursed his lips and began picking over the selections on his plate. The berry he settled on was ruby red and almost completely symmetrical, and he bit into it with zeal. The sour taste that filled his mouth was so opposite of what he expected that he gagged and spat it out, causing the women to burst out laughing again.

"So much for being selective," Tamara guffawed as she wiped tears from her face.

Sam blushed almost the same shade as the remnants of his unfortunate produce and ran his sleeve across his face.

"It's okay, Sam," Miranda said while she cleaned up the mess. "Sometimes, even the best, most perfect-looking fruit can be deceptive. Here." She passed him a lumpy, bruised-looking strawberry from her own bowl. "Try this one."

He glared at her but accepted the berry and took a bite. A sharp sweetness filled his senses, and he closed his eyes to savor the sensation. When he opened them, he smiled. "Much better, Mom. Thanks. Maybe I had better let you pick them for me from now on."

She gave him a tiny, satisfied nod and turned to survey the remaining berries. "I trust in your ability to learn from mistakes and make your own decisions."

"Humph," Sam grunted and went for an apple slice. Tamara, who had watched the exchange through narrowed eyes, tossed her curls in a dismissive gesture in an attempt to hide the fact that she felt left out.

"Well, I don't know what you two are talking about, but it certainly isn't this delicious feast. I haven't had real food since the radishes we grew in the lab last summer, and those don't even compare." Sam was about to protest, but she held up her hand. "I know—you don't want to talk about it, at least not in front of me. It's fine. I'm just happy to be here, though." She looked at Miranda. "Dad will be sorry he missed this."

Miranda exchanged a glance with Sam before she reached into a cabinet and grabbed a container. "I'll pack some up for him. I expect the weather created some challenges for him on campus."

"Yeah, one of the residential buildings flooded. He doesn't mind working late, though. He's just happy to have the job." Tamara gave Miranda a look of gratitude bordering on adulation.

Miranda brushed off the comment with a wave of her hand. "All I did was connect him with the university's maintenance branch. They knew your father's value as soon as they saw his portfolio. They might not have said so to him, but a few of them agreed with me that it is a shame that the Tiering system no longer values sculpture or visual arts."

"Or any kind of art for that matter," Sam interjected and nudged Tamara with his elbow. Like her father, a sculptor-turned-facility manager, she had artistic tendencies but was forced to prepare for positions within the Tiering system, which no longer included any jobs associated with the creative arts.

Tamara felt a tremor run through her at the physical contact, and she moved her knee to touch his. He stiffened in response and moved his leg away. He liked Tamara—liked her very much, in fact—but given his odd appearance and introversion, he lacked confidence in his ability to attract women, especially someone as outgoing and adorable as Tamara.

To cover her discomfiture at his apparent direction, Tamara scooted her stool toward Miranda. "Just the same, Dad and I know what we owe you, Dr. Richmond. We'd probably be indigent or dead without your help."

"While that may be true," Miranda said with a neutral expression, "I still thank my lucky stars that Hamid brought you into my free clinic all those years ago. You were very sick, but I was—and am—amazed at how quickly your body adapted to fight off that plague variant. Your genes helped us save thousands of lives that year, Tam." She walked over to Tamara and put her hand gently on her shoulder. "And you and your father helped make our family whole again. We are so much better off for having you in our lives." She leaned over and kissed Tamara's curls and then looked at Sam to prompt him.

Tamara's blush deepened, but with pleasure instead of embarrassment. "You see, Sam," she said pointedly, "you need me. Your mom just said so."

Sam held out his hands in supplication and grinned. "Conceded. With pleasure." He turned serious. "But at least one of us will have to learn to live without you."

Her brow furrowed in consternation. "What do you mean?"

Sam looked down and picked at his plate, unwilling to meet her eyes, and sighed. "Well, you see, I—um—I changed my mind about my Accessions bid."

The blood left her face as quickly as it had rushed in. "You didn't," she said flatly. "You wouldn't do something like that without telling me first."

"It was a recent change." *This is going to be more awkward than I anticipated.* He looked at his mother, who gave him a nod of encouragement, and then he faced Tamara. "I decided to make Capsule my first choice."

Tamara went very still, and her eyes smarted with tears of disappointment. "But we talked about this," she said when she recovered her voice. "You were going to work for your mother in Human Engineering here, and I was going to get into one of Reno's Tier I nutrition support positions for the Human Resiliency Program. If you get Capsule, there's zero chance we will be anywhere near each other. There are no capsules around here!" She pushed her plate away, wiped her tears, and crossed her arms over her chest as she glared between Sam and Miranda. "So much for needing me to be around."

"Hey," Sam said kindly. "Don't be like that. Do you really think I would just leave you?"

"I don't know what to think right now," she blurted. "Both of you just sitting here, talking over my head instead of—"

"Tamara," Miranda interrupted, "Capsule was on your bid list as well. Wasn't it?"

"Yes," she responded defiantly, "but more as wishful thinking. No one from the program even came to my interview. And you both know I wouldn't leave my father unless I had no other choice."

"Right," Sam agreed. It was true. With the exception of the Capsule program, every position Tamara expressed interest in was located in the Great Basin region. "But if my mom stays here—"

"I will ensure he is taken care of," Miranda promised, but she would not meet Tamara's eyes.

"That still doesn't solve the problem, though," Tam argued, "because I have no chance in hell of being offered Capsule."

"What if I were to tell you that I sent your radish project results to Capsule's agriculture directorate and that they were intrigued?"

Tamara stared at Miranda. "You did what? Wait a minute. How did you know I was interested in agriculture? I never said anything about it."

Miranda jerked her thumb at Sam. "He told me."

"Well, how did he know?" She scowled at him.

"Easy enough," he said lightly. "I do pay attention, you know. You've had a lot of dirt on your hands and plenty of messy uniforms lately. Plus, you have this smell…"

"Shut *up!*" she responded, mortified. "I do not smell. And I can't believe you noticed those things. You never mentioned them."

He shrugged. "I figured you would tell me when you were ready. And, frankly, I think it is a better fit for your interests, anyhow. You always get way more excited about playing in the dirt and growing things than experimenting with food supplements."

She gave him a punch on the arm that was halfway between a joke and a serious blow, and he rubbed the spot ruefully. "Fine, you win. You're right as usual. If by some miracle I get offered Capsule, I'll take it. That is," here she looked at Miranda, "as long as my father's job is safe."

"I'll do my best," Miranda agreed and then hastily changed the topic. "Now that Tamara is in on your plans, Sam, why don't you tell us both how you think your interview went?"

Sam returned to playing with his food as both women observed him closely. "The first part of it went well," he said nonchalantly before he looked up. "But to be honest, I could not get a read on Dr. Gage."

Tamara gaped at him, and Miranda drew in a sharp breath. "Stephan Gage interviewed you? In person?"

"In hologram, actually," Sam responded, puzzled at Miranda's response. "Apparently waiting until the last minute to interview was advantageous after all. My résumé was one of a handful he had left to review, and it caught his attention, or so he said."

Miranda's eyes narrowed, and her lips went in a straight line. "I didn't realize he was still doing interviews."

Sam leaned back and put his hands on the island. "I don't think he planned on doing any more this year."

"I'm sure he found you impressive," Miranda said neutrally and turned away to hide the tumult of feelings that jolted through her at the mention of Gage's name.

He exhaled loudly. "I'm confident my answers to his questions surprised him, but I don't know him well enough to assess whether he was pleased or repelled."

Miranda made a sound that Sam took for assent while Tamara asked, "What was he like?"

"Interesting," Sam responded. "Let me have a little more time to reflect on the experience and I can give you more details."

She smiled again, but warily. "That sounds more like you."

"At any rate, Mom, you can ask him about it when you get into your new role. I expect you'll be working pretty closely together." Sam scrutinized his mother for a response to this statement, but she turned around as her wristlet buzzed.

"Oh?" she said, absently, her mind elsewhere. "Right," she said. "Sorry guys, it's my replacement on the line. I have to take his call."

"It's okay, Mom. We'll be fine," Sam said. Even the few meals they were able to share were frequently interrupted by her work.

"Thanks, honey." She went to her soundproof work alcove and activated her terminal.

Tamara followed her with eyes full of concern. "That was weird. Is she okay?"

Sam looked at his mother. "I think she has a lot on her mind lately."

"What new role were you talking about?" Tamara asked.

Sam threw a few blueberries into his mouth. "I think she's still waiting for the official announcement before she tells anyone or—" a sudden realization hit him, "she could be getting the authorization right now. At any rate, it will be official before our Accessions Day, so you'll know soon enough."

Tamara sat back in her chair and crossed her arms again. "If you don't tell me now, I'll just ask when she's finished with the call."

"I'm surprised you haven't already," he mumbled, his mouth full of fruit.

"Don't be such a jerk, Sam. I'm worried about her and about you. You've both been behaving out of character tonight."

"I'm sorry, Tam." He sighed. "Really. Mom and I had a heart-to-heart after the Tunnel, and I realized I want to create my own path, independent of her, if possible. That doesn't mean I don't care about her or about you. I just needed my own—" He struggled to think of the word.

"Legacy," Tamara finished for him. "I've known that about you for a while. I just didn't see the Capsule thing coming." She rested her chin in her hands and turned her face toward his.

"Neither did I," he admitted, discomfited by the love and longing shining in her eyes. "I promise I won't hide anything like that from you again."

"You had better not," she said flippantly. "In the meantime, I will accept these delicacies—" she gestured toward the fruit, "as payment for my continued vigilance and goodwill." She waggled her eyebrows playfully at him to put him back at ease and snatched a strawberry from his plate. As he watched, she stuffed it into her mouth with a mischievous smile to mask her own frustration. "Delicious," she commented as she revealed a mouth full of reddened teeth.

Sam sputtered. *It is impossible to keep her spirits down for long.* "Agreed," he responded and passed her his plate.

CHAPTER SIX:

THE GIFT

Sam found himself in a room filled with fluorescent white light. A man dressed in black with silver-cropped hair stood next to him with a defiant expression on his face. He and Sam were fixated on the specter in front of them—a shadowed human form approaching through an opening that appeared with a rumble in one of the walls. It was the only dark spot in the otherwise blinding light. The backlit figure approached and reached toward Sam as a masked voice echoed through the chamber.

"Join us. This is your chance. Join us or unite with those who would destroy us all. The choice is yours."

The voice sounded familiar and friendly to Sam, but the man with him responded with contempt.

"No. His choice is mine, and I have already chosen." He turned toward Sam and, before the shadowy being could stop him, put Sam in a headlock and started to drag him out of the light. Sam felt the pressure of the arm on his larynx and choked. He could barely hear the figure's voice over the buzzing in his ears.

"Break away, Sam," it commanded. "Break away!"

Sam woke with a start. He was twisted onto one side, his blanket wrapped around his throat and midsection. As he disentangled himself, he puzzled over the familiar, faceless voice. *If only I had been able to stay in the dream a few more minutes, I could have identified it.*

He sighed, threw the blanket aside, and stretched, conscious of a mild headache. The dream's details faded as he remembered the other reason his stomach felt like it was full of tiny colliding particles. It was Accessions Day, and his anxiety about the future would either be replaced by hope, or it would increase as he contemplated a life of bland, hopeless drudgery.

Stop being so dramatic, Sam chastised himself. He was at or near the top of the pack of eligible candidates, and in any event, extreme outcomes were statistically unlikely. However, anything short of the Human Resiliency Program would be a severe blow to his self-worth and one from which he was unlikely to recover.

He tried to shake off some of those thoughts as he threw some of his daily water ration on his face and smoothed his short, spiky brown hair. With surprise, he heard his mother call him to breakfast. She normally spent mornings at her walk-in patient clinic for those without medical privileges before heading to the gene therapy lab at the university. She was rarely home when he awoke and often returned home well after he had consumed his evening ration. In fact, Sam mused as he dressed in his beige uniform, apart from the surprise dinner after the Tunnel, they had not shared a meal together in months.

Curious as to why she was home, Sam quickly tidied up his bunk and its adjacent washroom. He caught a quick glance of himself in the mirror. *Today may be the last day I'm ever in beige.* The thought helped steady his nerves as he moved into the galley.

Miranda stood behind the island, in the process of putting out two rations' worth of breakfast. She looked up and scrutinized Sam's face. "Good morning, honey. You don't look as if you slept very well."

"It's okay, Mom. Just nerves, I suppose. Nerves and strange dreams."

"Oh?" she asked and returned her focus to meal preparation, not that there was much to do other than set out plates of concentrated nutrient bars that crumbled almost as soon as they were touched.

Sam was not ready to share the contents of his dream just yet, so he redirected the conversation. "No patients this morning?"

Miranda sat down, shook her head, and smiled. "No, honey, of course not. Dr. Lin is taking my patients today." She hesitated and reached for his hand. "I wanted to see you off for your big day."

Sam flushed, muttered a nervous, "Thanks, Mom," and removed his hand to continue the process of breaking his breakfast into bite-sized chunks. He grimaced at the first spoonful that hit his tastebuds. Kelp. Again. The prime ingredient in most of their rations. *Better something in the stomach to settle the nerves,* he reminded himself.

On the next bite, he caught his mother looking at him and returned her gaze. She looked as if she had not slept at all, and her gray-streaked brown hair wisped around her face like repurposed plastic bedding. *Maybe Tam had a point,* he thought, reconsidering their conversation about Miranda. There was as yet no announcement about her new role, and he wondered if the strain of waiting for it was getting to her.

"Are you okay, Mom?" he asked after he choked down the kelp bar.

She looked up quickly, caught off guard, but recovered. "I'm fine, thanks, honey. I'm more concerned about you today, not that I'm worried about the outcome." She gave him a smile that did not quite reach her eyes and then turned away. When she looked back at him, her eyes shone with tears. "Your father would be so excited for you today."

"Would he?" Sam asked. He had never known his father, John, who was killed in an accident at work before his son's third birthday. Miranda had recently spoken about him more often, especially when she was trying to avoid questions about herself.

"Yes, he would. He saw greatness in you, even before you could walk. You were a quiet child, always watching and taking things in. He used to call you his 'little deep thinker.'" She smiled at the memory and, to Sam's surprise and embarrassment, brushed tears from her face.

Although he loved his mother, Sam knew she preferred to show her feelings in less obvious ways, and she rarely engaged in physical affection or emotion. Instead, she treated him as an adult, taught him, and let him share in her work over his school breaks. In fact, he often thought her work was her one true love, the substitute for the partner fate had so cruelly snatched from her nearly two decades ago.

"Thanks, Mom," he said, unsure of how to respond. This was new territory for him.

Miranda gave him one of her rare smiles. "It's okay, Sam. What I really wanted to say was that you have no reason to be nervous today."

Sam felt his stomach surge up into the back of his throat again at the reminder, and he pushed the rest of his food away. "No platitudes, please."

She sighed, nodded, and stood up. "Very well. I expect they are doing more harm than good right now." She hesitated. "Sam, just remember that whatever happens today does not define you. You have so many talents and so much heart that anyone would be lucky to have you as part of whatever they're working on. In fact, I expect that someday you will create enough options for yourself to choose your own path."

"Like you did, Mom?" His question dripped with sarcasm, and he instantly regretted his tone. Five years ago, Miranda had turned down an opportunity to work at a government medical facility even though it would have meant better opportunities for her to work on the things she really cared about. She had felt—and clearly was still—committed to her clinic patients and her work, but Sam also suspected she was unwilling to take a Tier demotion and reduce the privileges that allowed Sam access to the best education and care. As he matured, he recognized what a sacrifice it had been.

"Sorry," he said as he stood up. "That was childish of me. Please blame the stress of waiting for an outcome I no longer control."

Miranda muttered something along the lines of, "I cannot believe the pressure this system puts on our children," to herself before making strong eye contact with Sam. He felt as if she was trying to imprint her words and a part of herself on him. "You will always be the most important person in the world to me, regardless of what you do with your life."

She gave her words a moment to sink in. "Remember, you've worked alongside me on projects and challenges that even my peers would not risk their reputations on, and you performed magnificently. You have made it through every single test and every screening mechanism they could throw at you, and you refused to give up, even when everyone else was telling you that you should. Even if you were not my son, I would want you on my team. You just do not yet see yourself as the capable person or the capable leader I know you can be."

With a quick movement, she closed the distance between them and ruffled Sam's hair the way she used to do when he was a little boy. "That confidence comes with experience, as you will soon find out."

Sam stood there feeling awkward until she removed her hand, turned away, wiped the tears off her face, and cleared her throat. "I have something for you that I've been saving for a special occasion. It was your grandmother's."

She went to the small room off the galley where she slept. When she returned, she had an oval-shaped tin box in her hand. It was clearly meant to look like the paper-wrapped gifts from the more wasteful days he had read about.

Curious, he opened the box and pulled out a small pendant on a tiny chain that was too small to fit around his neck.

"The original chain broke," Miranda explained. "My mother donated it for smelting. The one on there was taken from her dog tags from her time as a space engineer. The necklace itself was a gift from her—ahem—from my father."

Sam noted the falter. Miranda's birth had caused a scandal. Her parents, both of whom were respected engineers at the same off-moon outpost, fell for each other. They failed to apply for a marriage license and certainly never received permission to have a child. Only his grandmother's renown and insistence had prevented a forced abortion.

He examined the pendant. It had a snowflake on the front of its silvery surface. He—and most of his generation—had never seen real snow.

"She grew up in Wyoming. Your grandmother loved the snow as a child, and she missed being able to ski and snowshoe." Miranda sounded wistful. "Check the other side."

Sam flipped the small metal disc over and saw a single, counterclockwise swirl. Along the bottom were the initials "S.R." Samantha Richmond.

Miranda continued, "My father was a space station construction engineer, but his first love was math, just as my mother was his first human love, or so she told me."

He recognized the symbology of the snowflake at once and remembered his own fascination with the fractal patterns in ice during his math and engineering courses. However, the flakes he studied were generated in a lab environment given the unavailability of real snow. As he examined the pendant more closely, he realized the faded grooves in the flake's imprint replicated the infinite fractal patterns inside one created by nature.

"It looks realistic. Doesn't it? Your grandfather had the pattern preserved from a real one during their last skiing trip together—the one they took after they were sent back to Earth for the transgression of my conception. He told my mother it was a representation of how perfect and infinite his love for her was."

Pretty sappy, thought Sam. Definitely not his line, but it worked on his grandmother. He flipped the disc back over and studied the coil on its back. From a distance, it looked plain enough, but the shape also seemed familiar. "A logarithmic spiral?" he asked.

"Exactly." Miranda beamed. "I knew you would figure that out pretty quickly." The smile faded, and she gave him another all-absorbing look. "This is yours now, Sam. Hang onto it until you find the right time to pass it on. You'll know when to do it and who to give it to." She reached over and embraced Sam tightly, taking him by surprise.

He stood still for a moment and then gently squeezed her back before breaking off the embrace. To his dismay, he saw her eyes welling up again.

"I have to get going, Mom. The electrotrain to the assembly area will be here soon and Tam is probably waiting for me."

"Don't worry about me," she said, brushing the tears away. "I'm in a sentimental mood today seeing you ready to embark on your adult life." She pressed her lips together in a tight smile. "Yes, you had better leave soon. The pollution index today is terrible—lots of nasty bits in the area with the smoke from that latest—ah—wildfire."

She moved out of his way so he could enter the decontamination chamber and put on his protective suit, and she watched as he put the pendant on his wrist. Sam waved to her through the window of the air-locked chamber and saw her wave back as if she was trying to take a picture of him to store in her memory. Then he turned to the exterior hatch, exited, and sealed the door behind him.

CHAPTER SEVEN:

THE DISTURBANCE

Sam heard the hiss of the airlock seal behind him. The pendant clanked against his wrist, still warm from his mother's touch. It was hazy, and, according to his protective suit's monitor, it was a balmy 107 degrees Fahrenheit. *Cool for June,* he thought, as he looked west. The previous night's storm dissipated over the mountains, and he made a mental note to clean out the airlock and decontamination chamber over the weekend.

If I am still here, he realized, startled. Depending on how the day went, he might already be lodged according to the billeting and rationing scale of his new position by then.

Sam swallowed convulsively as his stomach churned. The familiar row of reinforced fiberglass bungalows suddenly seemed like soldiers standing to attention as part of a farewell cordon, and it occurred to him how much he had taken the privilege of private housing—and privacy more generally—for granted. Miranda's occupation ensured that they had the best of everything. Ordinary citizens lived in repurposed data centers and "shopping malls" that contained compartmentalized living spaces based on family size. Most counted themselves fortunate to be billeted in private bunks with communal dining and washroom facilities. He shuddered at the thought.

He continued toward the electrotrain platform, barely noticing the omnipresent security forces. They were responsible for protecting the housing areas and transportation hubs. Their presence had gradually increased after the last uprising. One of the guards eyed Sam suspiciously as he turned from the elevators and climbed the stairs. Sam did not notice. For him, the stairs provided a good opportunity for additional exercise, especially in his protective suit. Between his Accessions training and unpalatable weather, there were so few days when he did not have to wear it outside that Sam had almost forgotten what it was like to move around without the extra load.

As he crested the stairs, he observed an unusually high number of security force personnel on the platform, some of whom wore the distinctive black, gray, and white camouflage of the Interior Police. A movement in the periphery of his vision caused him to look upward. Overhead, a V-shaped formation of nine emergency services aircraft hummed and gleamed as they moved south toward clouds of dense gray smoke that rose in columns from near the city center.

"Probably another wildfire," a woman behind him commented. Sam turned and glanced at her. Her protective suit had the burnt orange insignia of the solar farm plant, and her lined face marked her as one of its panel maintainers. The relentless sun wreaked havoc with complexions.

"You think so?" her similarly clad male companion replied.

"I saw something about it in our news feed before I left the building."

"Oh," the man said, unconcerned. "I hope they get control of it quickly. The last one turned into a real firestorm."

Sam scrutinized the smoke while he walked toward the queue, and he examined the disappearing aircraft again. He thought he saw the glint of ultrasonic cannons on the vessels' undersides, which, from a distance, could have been mistaken for striping.

That is no wildfire, he was certain. But he remembered the conversations with his mother and, more recently, Stephan Gage.

The passengers stood in line for the electrotrain and huddled between the guards like trapped roaches. Some turned as he approached, and a short, squat figure broke out from among them and waved.

"Hey, Sam!" The voice was muffled through layers of plastic and Kevlar. Even so, Sam heard his own nervousness echoed in the familiar voice that hailed him, but hers was masked by a layer of indefatigable enthusiasm.

"Hello, Tam." He felt his mouth smile despite his nerves and other concerns.

"I was hoping we would be on the train together," she gushed. "I stopped by your bungalow this morning, but I figured you and your mom would want some privacy." The caution in her wide brown eyes suggested she questioned that decision.

"You were right about that," he reassured her but decided to hold back the information about his mother's odd behavior. "But I'm glad we get to travel to the ceremony together anyhow."

"Oh, good. I knew I did the right thing, but I'm so happy you're here now. I don't think I could stand being alone on the ride in without going crazy. How are you feeling?"

"Nervous," he admitted. *In more ways than one.* "You?"

She tossed her head, causing her protective hood to smack her in the face, and then smirked at her blunder. "Kind of like I'm about to find out whether I have a deadly disease or just a cold."

They were interrupted by a cool, soothing voice. "The train to Great Basin University and City Center is arriving. Please stand clear of the platform edge and wait for passengers to disembark before boarding." The electrotrain slid into the station with a gentle, rhythmic hum. Sam and Tamara stood back to allow a handful of oxygen-suit-clad people to shuffle out of the train's doors as well as some additional armed guards. At the sight of the guards, Tamara latched on to his arm, and he was forced to drag her aboard with him to one of the remaining open booths in the car.

She gaped at the additional guards in the car as he helped her to a seat, and she squeaked with fear as the doors, which were monitored by additional security force personnel, closed. He turned to her, raised his eyebrows with meaning, and removed his helmet. She followed his lead and looked around nervously below sweat-dampened curls. Sam wiped the condensation from his helmet's transparent hood and motioned anxiously for her to do the same, but she fidgeted in her seat as she looked around at the squad of guards in their car.

"Why are so many of them on the train today?" she asked in a whisper so loud she might as well have shouted.

Sam saw the nearest guard, a bald, muscular man with a face ugly enough to turn a gorgon to stone, catch the gist of Tamara's comment, and he shook his head slightly in warning. Her lips trembled when she realized she was being watched. Sam laid his hand over hers in a calming gesture, and she gripped his so tightly in response that he gave an involuntary cry.

The gorgon-guard was at their booth in a flash, rifle at the ready. "What seems to be the problem here, folks?"

Sam inhaled and looked him in the eye just like his mother had taught him. *Your calm will make them calm,* she had murmured after they witnessed a brutal altercation between a distraught citizen and an overzealous policeman. *Be polite, be courteous, be serene. Do not show that you are afraid, and you will not be afraid.*

"My apologies, sir. We are both a little edgy about today." He pointed to the collar of his beige uniform, which was just visible over the edge of his protective gear.

Gorgon peered closer, realized they were students, and gave a satisfied grunt. "Well, be careful, you two. Many dissenters out there would love to make a mess out of the Accessions events." He jerked his free hand in the direction of the window and glared at Tamara. "We take all acts of violence seriously. This is not the time to be messing around, young lady."

"Yes. I mean, yes, sir," she stuttered.

Sam recognized how close she was to hysteria. "Of course, sir," he said in his most submissive tone. *And always make them feel that they are in control.* "We will be more careful. Thank you for the reminder and thanks for keeping us safe."

Gorgon stepped back, mollified. "You're welcome. It's my job." He gave Sam a tight smile, returned to his position at the head of the car, and muttered something unintelligible to the receiver inside his helmet, which caused his comrades to return to their posts at the doors and windows.

Tamara continued to tremble. "So," Sam said to distract her, "Mom and I talked about you again yesterday, and she got some good news."

The ploy worked as expected. She stopped trembling and looked at him with eyes that glinted with anticipation. "What kind of news?"

He grinned. "Guess."

She rolled her eyes. "Oh, come on, Sam! By the time I get it right, we'll both have our Accessions results. Just tell me for heaven's sake." When he crossed his arms and kept smiling at her, she became irritated. "Are you seriously going to make me wait until the ceremony to find out?"

"Why don't you try the process of elimination? We have at least twenty minutes before the university stop."

She opened her mouth to retort but was interrupted by the screech of brakes. The electrotrain slowed and shuddered to a halt so quickly they were thrust forward into the divider between their booth and the car's door. The other passengers cried out in surprise and alarm.

"Everyone, remain in your seats!" Gorgon yelled the command and then issued instructions to his team. Sam caught a quick glance out the window of clusters of crumbled, unsealed buildings and makeshift fiberglass weatherproofing before metal shields shuttered his view.

"We're in your old neighborhood," he murmured to Tamara as the lead guard ordered the passengers to be quiet. Sam complied but kept his senses alert as he put a protective arm around his stunned friend.

Tamara and her father had come from one of Reno's indigent zones, places where people with no employment and, consequently, no formal government benefits subsisted. Some of them had failed to assess into the bottom Tiers due to poor performance during testing, misconduct, or poor health. Others, like Hamid Ashraf, who had been a professional sculptor, were downgraded out of the Tiering system when their professions were no longer deemed necessary. Members of these communities had few options. The lucky ones reentered the bidding process and assessed into new positions that were usually lower down in the Tiering system. Most, however, were not so fortunate; they were forced to squabble for temporary jobs, join the ranks of the vagrant population, or rebel against the system that had rejected them.

Sam and Tamara heard some loud thuds from outside the car, and Sam smelled smoke—not the woodsmoke of wildfire or the sweetish smell of burning fiberglass. This was the acrid, chemical smell of explosives. The train shook with the vibrations of a struggle between man and nature. *Or, rather, between man and man.* Sam thought he heard distant yells and screams.

"Those poor people," Tamara murmured and buried her head into his shoulder. He stroked her hair absently while he listened to the noises and pieced together a picture of the disturbance outside.

The din quieted to an ominous silence after a few moments of muffled thumping. A message came through Gorgon's headset. "Nothing to worry about here, folks," he announced. "The fire from this morning just jumped the tracks in front of us, that's all. Our emergency services have contained the worst of the blaze, and we will proceed to the next stop momentarily. Please remain silent for the remainder of your journey today."

Calming music and the scent of lavender flooded the cars as the electrotrain crept forward. Tamara lifted her tear-stained face to look at Sam, who gave her an encouraging nod and a smile. She sighed, laid her head on his shoulder again, and closed her eyes.

As the train accelerated, he felt her grip his hand tightly as if it was a true lifeline to safe harbor instead of a mirage.

CHAPTER EIGHT:

THE CEREMONY

They proceeded in silence from the train to the university's auditorium flanked by a cordon of more armed guards. Hundreds of other hopefuls flooded in from all directions in the same eerie silence.

Tamara pulled at Sam's arm so hard it was all he could do to propel the two of them forward toward the entrance. There, they were pried apart so they could be scanned for weapons and explosives. Once inside, both removed their helmets. Tamara turned towards the sound of whispered conversations that echoed throughout the cavernous antechamber.

"Is security normally like this?" she asked.

Sam shrugged. "I've never attended the ceremony before either." He saw she was still trembling, so he added, "It's okay. I'm sure we're safe in here."

"If you say so." She looked dubious as she arched her neck to see over the people. "It looks like I have to go over to the 'A' section for check-in. Hopefully, we'll be seated near each other. If not, can I meet you back at this entrance afterward so we can ride back together?"

"Of course," Sam agreed. "I'll see you soon. Good luck!"

"You, too." She waved and bounced off toward the right. Sam looked up, saw a giant letter "M," and turned left until he found "R" and lined up behind two others at the desk.

"Name?" the woman there asked without looking up.

"Samuel J. Richmond."

She checked her terminal. "Parents?"

"Dr. Miranda S. Richmond."

The woman looked up and raised an eyebrow in disbelief. She checked her terminal again and shook her head. "Very well. Proof of identification, please."

Sam bent over, placed his forehead into the semi-circular scanner, and felt it warm against his clammy skin. The device gave a pleasant tone as the terminal screen flashed green.

"Confirmed," the woman said, surprised. She assessed Sam's appearance again, this time with a hint of awe. "You are in section thirty-two, row seven. Please proceed to the suit stowage area and then to your seat. The ceremony will begin in approximately twenty minutes."

Here we go. Sam cringed and nodded. After he stowed his suit, he entered the auditorium at entrance thirty-two. The dimly lit bowl teemed with sounds of excited voices edged with unease. Row seven was near the center of the stage, and Sam waited with impatience for the others in front of him to file off to their own rows. As he turned to find his seat, he tripped over a foot and would have fallen flat on his face had not strong hands caught him and hauled him to his feet.

"Watch it there, Richmond! Wait until you actually get your results before you decide to pass out."

Sam looked up toward the booming voice that went with the hands and saw a square-jawed face topped with golden-brown curls. "Thanks," he gasped. "Hector Ramirez. Right?"

"The very same." Hector smiled and returned to his seat. "You must have read my name tag." Unlike everyone else around him, Hector oozed confidence and relaxation as he gestured to Sam to take the seat next to him.

There was no help for it. Even though Sam did not want company, it would have been rude to move down the row. He gave an inward sigh and sat stiffly. He was about to switch on his seat's display when Hector tapped him on the shoulder.

"Hey, I think you dropped this." Hector held out a small silver object. "It was like this when I picked it up," he added in an apologetic manner.

Sam took his mother's pendant and noticed the flimsy chain was indeed broken. The silver disc, however, remained intact. "Thank you," Sam said, relieved that nothing worse had happened. "It's a family heirloom."

"I figured as much. Cool pattern on the back, though. I'm keeping my good luck talisman here." Hector patted his left breast pocket and put his hands behind his head. "Ugh, I wish they would just get to it already. The suspense is killing me."

Sam was not sure whether Hector was joking, so he murmured assent and pressed a button on the arm of his seat. A translucent display appeared that read:

Richmond, Samuel J.

Employment Offers Pending

He saw others in his section activate their displays but could only read his own. Looking around, he observed a handful of empty seats amid students attired in the browns, taupes, and beiges of the academies.

Probably more disappearances, he mused. *The numbers are increasing.*

His eyes were drawn to the stage as the lights over it glowed brighter. Armed men and women in blacks and grays edged the six-foot-high platform. Three chairs sat at its center with a small podium off to the side. Swaths of nearly transparent netting hung over the stage—the optical enhancers, Sam realized.

Someone waved frantically from the adjacent section. Sam looked over at Tamara and gave her a small salute in acknowledgment. She returned his tepid smile and mouthed "good luck" before taking her seat.

Hector followed Sam's gesture and gave him a thoughtful look. "Your girlfriend?" he asked.

"No," Sam responded automatically. "But she is my closest friend."

"Oh." Hector's brow furrowed. "What's the difference?"

To his surprise and dismay, Sam felt warm color rush to his cheeks and was saved from answering by a booming voice.

"Ladies and gentlemen, please find your seats. The ceremony will begin momentarily."

The entire auditorium went dark as the voice spoke, and Sam, like many others around him, had to remind himself to breathe.

When the lights came back on, they illuminated the stage like a beacon. And there, seated between Governor Leticia Rand and her pudgy Regional Accessions Director, was Dr. Stephan Gage. The audience gave a collective gasp. Gage's presence could only mean one thing: some of their number had assessed into the Capsule Project.

Sam felt a thrill of anticipation and his mind raced with possibilities. Gage was in his interview and surely his presence now suggested that... *Wait, he may have been in other interviews as well and hinted as much.* So engrossed was he in these ruminations that he did not notice the nervous glances the governor darted at Gage from her dark eyes when she moved to the podium.

"Candidates, faculty, and citizens of the greater Washoe Valley. Welcome to the fifty-first annual Accessions Day. As you know, this is a momentous occasion for our young people as they embark on their adult lives and a second chance for many others. This year's competition was intense..."

Sam tuned out the platitudes and looked around his seating area. He recognized many of his classmates and others he had tested with like Hector. He comforted himself with the fact that, of the thousands present today, only a handful were even eligible for the Human Resiliency Program. The relief was short-lived, however. Self-doubt, Sam's constant sidekick, crept in when he saw the rapt, hopeful expressions on the faces around him.

Governor Rand finished, having transitioned from inanities to a long list of Dr. Gage's accomplishments. *He hardly needs the recitation, though,* Sam thought. As the leader and public face of Capsule, Gage was a target for admiration, envy, and, on occasion, rage, which at least partially explained the additional security around the facility.

Gage launched out of his chair to the podium after the governor's lengthy introduction and signaled for the lights to dim.

"Good morning, candidates. You all know who I am, and I know at least a hundred or so of you requested a position in my program. Our unprecedented achievements over the past few years have been in part thanks to the new talent and new ideas we bring into our capsules during each Accessions cycle. Some of the top applicants are from this region, which is one reason I am here."

Gage paused and looked around the auditorium to give his words emphasis and took a moment to enjoy the appreciative murmurs that bounced off of the acoustically enhanced walls. He let his eyes linger on Sam's section and Sam wondered whether it was coincidence. Behind Gage, the optical nets merged and glowed before they produced a three-dimensional image of a large transparent dome crisscrossed with a triangular pattern of supports and solar receivers.

"I also wanted to use this occasion to make an important announcement. Capsule is about to embark upon an exciting new chapter, and this year's selectees will be among the first in the country—if not the world—to join us in that endeavor."

The murmurs turned into rumbles of excitement, and Gage raised his hand for silence. "We are now in the process of expanding our current operations, which consists of several dozen capsules capable of housing a thousand to fifteen hundred personnel. The elemental construction for the first set of our Phase III capsules is now complete, and our new prototype, I am happy to say, will be able to accommodate up to five thousand people when fully operational. It is also more durable and will be able to withstand the various types of extreme weather patterns that occur in each of the derelict zones, including the harshest temperatures, the most violent storms, and the marshiest of floodplains."

The simulated capsule blurred and then returned, enlarged, on the backdrop of a barren plain. The audience made awed noises as the capsule was successively battered by fire, cyclones, a hurricane, and acid rain. While it emerged bruised, it remained intact.

Gage waited for the simulation to finish, and the auditorium around the stage darkened again. The audience went silent, and Sam wondered how many of them, like him, were considering the pros and cons of accepting what were likely to be very tough living conditions in an extraordinary enterprise. But he also felt the pull of the offer to be part of history.

Gage gave his audience an appreciative nod. "The capsules that survive the Phase III proof of concept will become models for those who will eventually provide a future for our country's population and, in time, other areas of the world. The people who help make them work will become legends in and after their own time, and they will have earned their place in history."

While Gage spoke, Sam's stomach fell into his feet. He wondered whether he would even make the cut for Capsule at all now because of the physical challenges involved. Those had been his weakest points in an otherwise stellar packet.

"Those offered Capsule Phase II or Phase III are invited to join me for an informational briefing immediately following receipt of their Accessions results. You will join my personal security staff here at the stage, and they will escort you to another area of this facility. I look forward to meeting those of you we've hand-selected for the opportunity of a lifetime. Thank you for your attention."

Instead of resuming his seat, Gage walked to the edge of the stage and disappeared into the darkness.

The lights came back on, and the auditorium rippled with suppressed anxiety as the Regional Accessions director stood up and moved to the podium.

"Ahem. Quiet please." The noise died down, but the room strummed with tension. Sam's hands moistened.

"I am delighted to announce that most candidates in our region received one of their top three choices—an unprecedented number."

That is a lie. That outcome is not statistically possible given the published request numbers, Sam mused.

"This," the director continued, "speaks well of the quality of our system and, more importantly, the quality of our candidates. Please turn your attention to your displays. Your results will appear momentarily."

Sam looked back at his display and closed his eyes. Bizarrely, he found himself wishing for a surprise—that he would be offered something completely out of the blue. But that thought lasted less than a second as shouts of joy and groans brought him back into the present. He opened his eyes and was confronted with his results, which read:

Richmond, Samuel J. Northwest Division

Employment Offer:	**Position:**	**Tier:**	**Designation**
Capsule Program, Phase II, Midgard	Primary:	HRP	Active
Human Engineering Program, Northwest Division	Alternate 1:	HRP	Alternate
Capsule Program, Phase III, Southwest Division	Alternate 2:	HRP	Waitlist

Decision Period:
30 Days

He read them again, trying to absorb the words and what they meant. He was astonished and disappointed, and he looked around to see if anyone could read it on his face. He saw both joy and anguish as well as people who, like him, were shocked and dumbstruck. And, Sam realized, had he been a primary selectee for Phase III, he would have joined one of the celebratory groups. Midgard was the flagship of the Capsule Project, and, until five minutes ago, it would have been his top choice. But now the position felt diminished in light of what Gage had said about Phase III.

Sam's stomach churned, and he read his results again. Why had he been given the full thirty days to respond even though he was waitlisted for Phase III? *Perhaps I could ask Dr. Gage about it during the orientation session*, Sam thought as he moved toward the guards as directed and saw Hector there.

"Sam, Sam!" He turned and saw Tamara shoving her way through the crowds attempting to exit toward the stage. Next to him, Hector, too, turned.

"Oh, Sam," she said, throwing herself at him, "I just knew you'd get Capsule if you asked for it! I'm so happy for you. And you'll never guess what I got!"

He was about to tell her not to wait for him as he had an informational briefing to attend when flurried movements from the security team caught his attention.

The guard nearest him spoke into his receiver in a low, urgent voice and then motioned for other guards to move around the stage. Then he turned to the small group of candidates, held out his arms, and made a pumping motion with them as he cried, "All of you, get on the ground right now!"

Sam, like most of the candidates, stood still and stared.

"I said now, you—"

Before the head guard finished speaking, the auditorium shook violently as a deafening rumble moved through it like a tidal wave of sound. With it came a cloud of dust, debris, and a smothering force that flattened Sam and everyone around him to the ground.

CHAPTER NINE:

THE REQUEST

The ringing in Sam's ears dulled the sounds of the cries and breakage around him. He coughed out some dust and felt the pressure of something—or someone—on top of him when he tried to move. The weight shifted as the body on top of him rolled away, and Sam moved gingerly to his feet. Pain shot through his knee as someone steadied him.

"Sam," Tamara said in a shaky voice. "Are you okay?"

He coughed out some more dust as he responded, "I think so. What about you?"

Tamara's hair was covered in dust, and her face was either pale or soiled with debris. "I've felt better, but I'm in one piece. This guy," she pointed to a grubby Hector, who assisted another unfortunate to their feet, "protected me when the blast came."

Sam tried to focus. "You heard something detonate?"

"I don't know. Actually," she paused, "now that you mention it, there wasn't really an explosion per se, just a lot of noise and vibrations, and I felt sick to my stomach right before we were knocked down."

"Quiet!" yelled an armed guard with a burn that ran from his left ear down his neck in a strange, hook-like shape. "All of you candidates who can walk line up behind me."

The seven ambulatory prospects shuffled into a line and followed the scarred guard into a dark corridor, led by the light at the end of the guard's rifle. Sam fell in line behind Hector, and Tamara grabbed his hand for reassurance.

In what felt like an hour—but was actually only a minute or so—the group squinted in the light of a small room that seemed oddly untouched after the chaos from above.

Dr. Gage was speaking in low tones to a large, muscular man dressed in black. "No, I do not think it was a bomb," Sam heard him say. "Yes, the data is coming your way. The team here is working on it. Oh, and Castanada—that candidate we discussed last week—is a no-show. You were right about him."

Sam strained his ears to hear the other side of the conversation but was only able to make out the sounds of a male voice.

"Look, the recruits are here, so I will touch base with you later." After a pause, Dr. Gage nodded. "I have a meeting with her after the ceremony." Another pause. "Yes, of course. I am confident he will accept. Leave it with me. Midgard One out."

By the time he finished speaking, the still-dazed candidates were seated. Gage gave them a satirical smile. "Well, that was exciting. I hope you appreciate the lengths we went to in order to ensure that your Accessions ceremony was truly something special."

"The lengths we all went to, sir," added a thirty-ish man with raven hair, olive skin, and a medium build in an upbeat tone. Gage gave him an appreciative gesture and handed him his tablet.

Hector was the only candidate who smiled in response. Sensing the mood, Gage assumed a more serious expression.

"Welcome, Capsule nominees. I expect this experience has shaken you, but given your psychological testing scores, I know all of you have the capacity to calm yourselves under duress. I will allow you a few moments to do just that while I consult with my security team." He gave the group a curt nod, clapped the black-haired man on the shoulder, and exited followed closely by the man with the hooked scar.

Sam watched as the others closed their eyes to practice their deep breathing techniques, and he did the same. As his fear subsided, his curiosity arose. *What the hell is going on today?* While he ran through scenarios, he felt Tamara squeeze his hand, which she had not relinquished since they lined up. Startled, he turned to her.

"Tam, what are you doing here?"

She gaped at him and then collected herself. "I was trying to tell you before we were knocked down, but I got offered an Agricultural Engineering position in Capsule Phase III, Southwest Division. Isn't that awesome? I never imagined I'd get in. Which region are you in?"

"Midgard," Sam said flatly as he tried to process the fact that the middle-of-the-road Tamara had assessed into a premier program whereas he, at the top of his peer group, was only Phase II. *Mom did her job a little too well,* he thought, and then beat back the jealousy that threatened to make those thoughts into words he could not take back.

"Oh, Sam! That's the flagship. That is great! Aren't you excited? Your mom will be thrilled, too."

"Yes, you're right," he acknowledged in the same, cool tone.

Her face fell, and she looked down. "I guess we won't be together after all, though."

Sam was at a loss for words. He wished his disappointment had more to do with Tamara as a friend rather than

Tamara as competition, but that was not his nature. "Yes, that is unfortunate," he said flatly.

"Well, to me Midgard sounds amazing," Hector interrupted and took the seat next to Tamara. "I also got offered Southwest. I'm Hector Ramirez. And you are?" He looked between Tamara and Sam.

"Tamara Ashraf," she responded, "but most of my friends call me Tam. Hey, I think I've seen you before. Weren't you the guy who went through the Tunnel right before Sam? You were soooo fast!"

"Yes, that was me." Hector smiled, and his dimples matched hers.

The two of them struck up a conversation that Sam heard little of as others chimed in. He was mortified when he realized he was the only person of the seven who was not Phase III and was uncertain how to explain his dilemma to Miranda. With a start, he realized that his mother was probably frantic with worry at this point. He whipped out his wristlet to send her a quick note, but its screen was black. *Perhaps I broke it when I fell?*

"Mine is not working either," Hector said and held up his own.

Of course. "They probably have some sort of signal inhibitor," Sam said.

Gage returned and the candidates went quiet while he observed them. "Your wristlets will do you no good in here. The information I am about to disclose to you is confidential. If you choose to stay for the briefing, you must commit to a binding agreement that you will not discuss this material with anyone. Should you mention any of this information—even by mistake—we will know, and you will be detained."

The apprehension in the room was palpable. Everyone knew what "detention" meant—hard labor or vagrancy for the rest of one's natural life at best and an early demise regardless.

"Consider that little event in the auditorium as an introduction to what happens when people panic and leak critical information," Gage continued. "If you decide to join us in the Capsule program, you will not have the luxury of re-learning this lesson. You have ten minutes to decide whether this kind of environment is for you, and all of you must remain silent until everyone has made their decision. Time begins—now."

Gage placed his hand on a new tablet, this one silver instead of black. The candidates' wristlets vibrated. Sam quickly scanned the agreement on his screen. The last sentence was a simple question: *Do you accept the conditions of secrecy as described?* Below it was the option to select "yes" or "no." He looked up and met Gage's stare and saw the Capsule Director's eyes crinkle with amusement. Without breaking eye contact, Sam lowered his finger onto the "yes" button and watched Gabe's smile lines deepen.

A chair scraped the floor as one of the women present sighed, stood up, and made for the door. Gage nodded to one of his guards who took her wristlet. She looked as if she was about to protest but stopped when she caught Gage's icy glare.

"You'll get it back shortly," he said and gestured for the guards to remove her.

Over the next few minutes, Sam observed one other person opt-out and wondered about their cost-benefit calculus. What would cause them to leave a tremendous opportunity, even if they did not know it was one of the only prospects for a reasonable lifespan?

"Good!" Gage exclaimed, and Sam jumped slightly in his seat. "Finished with over two minutes to spare. Clearly, you are all capable of making a timely and monumental choice." The black-haired man entered with a brisk walk and another smile for Gage. "My assistant, Don, will now collect your wristlets. They will be returned to you at the conclusion of our discussion."

At Gage's signal, Don held out a tray. The candidates passed it around, placing their wristlets on it. Sam was the last to do so, and the sight reminded him of the manacles on those detained by the Interior Police.

Once Don exited with his tray, Gage palmed into a scanner on the table. Optic netting lowered from the ceiling and glowed before it wove itself together to form an enormous three-dimensional map of North America with forty-or-so-interconnected blue dots spread across United States territory. One larger dot, located just outside of the National Capital Region, pulsed like a heart valve. *Midgard,* thought Sam.

"The dots on this map indicate the approximate locations of our operational capsules, each capable of hosting up to one-thousand personnel," Gage began. "These active capsules represent Phase II of our plan to provide sustainable living space for hundreds of thousands of people over the next eighty years."

Interesting, Sam thought. He knew the actual locations of the capsules were a carefully guarded secret—for their own protection—but he wondered that Gage would present a visual like this to those who were still not officially part of the program.

New dots emerged in far larger numbers, this time in green. Some replaced the blue dots, while others stood alone, dispersed throughout the southern and coastal areas of the United States that were no longer habitable.

"These are approximate locations for our Phase III capsules, though only four of those sites are baseline operational," Gage continued."Make no mistake—these conditions will test even the hardiest of you in ways you have neither experienced nor imagined. Therefore, those of you offered Phase III will have a full month to make your final decision. The regional Accessions directors will hold your alternate positions until that thirty-day period is up unless, of course, you decide to accept sooner." Here, Gage flashed a mouth full of white, straight teeth.

The map vanished as it was replaced by a digital representation of a large silver and white analog clock. The hour hand neared the twelve and the minute hand was just past the eleven. "Do any of you recognize this?" he asked.

"Isn't that the Doomsday Clock, sir?" Hector asked, fascinated.

"Exactly," Gage agreed. "Now, Mr. Ramirez, please tell me what time it is and what it means."

"About four minutes to midnight," Hector responded confidently. "The time means that our civilization is very close to destroying itself, and I believe this is the same time it's shown since the end of the Third World War."

"Excellent. That is exactly what I would expect you to believe right now," Gage responded. He drew a small circle on top of the scanner with his finger. The movement caused the minute hand to move until it was almost parallel with the hour hand.

"Ladies and Gentlemen, what you see here is the actual state of affairs. Our world is less than ten seconds from midnight. The Earth is dying far faster than our efforts to stop it."

Everyone but Sam gasped with dismay, and Gage paused to let the message sink in. "We expect most forms of life on the Earth's surface to go extinct in a matter of decades, and we estimate we have less than thirty years to make Capsule a success if we want to preserve human life."

The clock disappeared and the lights returned. "Our government and like-minded members of the international community are doubling down on Human Resiliency efforts as a result, and Capsule is the farthest along of its projects. However, Our Phase III prototypes are behind schedule, and we're counting on fresh blood and fresh ideas to help us accelerate our efforts." Gage gave the group an appraising, poignant look.

"I want all of you, whether you are a primary or alternate for Phase III, to think carefully before committing. We cannot afford to lose good people or time at this juncture. The opportunities to learn and grow in Capsule are limitless, but we will not tolerate mediocrity or failure. Defectors will be dealt with in the most extreme measures possible."

Sam shuddered inwardly as Gage continued. "Don's contact information is being programmed into your wristlets as we speak, and he can answer any questions you might have during the decision period. Those he cannot answer will, of course, come to me."

As if on cue, Don returned bearing his tray. "You are dismissed," Gage said. "But I'd like Mr. Richmond to remain behind for a private chat."

Everyone turned toward Sam, who remained in his seat. Tamara met his eyes and sucked on her lower lip before being ushered out the door with the others.

Once the door closed, Gage motioned for Sam to join him at the head of the table. "I bet you are wondering why you did not get Phase III," he said when Sam was seated.

"Yes, sir," he admitted.

Gage suddenly looked tired and far older than his fifty years. "May I call you Sam?" he asked.

Stunned, Sam sputtered, "Of course, sir."

Gage folded his hands under his chin and scrutinized the young man's dark brown hair and murky hazel eyes. "You look like her—like Miranda. Not your coloring, of course, but your features are nearly identical, that little smirk of yours in particular."

"You know my mother?" Suddenly, Miranda's reaction to Gage's presence in Sam's interview made sense, though it also felt like a betrayal. *She never mentioned the relationship to me.*

Now it was Gage's turn to be surprised. "She and I were classmates at Midwest University, though we have not been in touch for—for quite some time. I am shocked she hasn't mentioned the connection before now."

"As am I," Sam agreed. *And I will have to ask her why she hid that information from me.*

Gage leaned forward. "Anyhow, I will get to the point. Sam, I need someone like you on my team working at the headquarters with me, not in some outer region battling the elements. You've got an impressive résumé, but your interview revealed a glimpse of some extraordinary abilities that none of our screening tests revealed. And," he joked, "I know you have fortitude. I think you're the only candidate in history to go through the Tunnel five times."

Sam blushed but remained mystified. *Where is this leading?*

"I can see I am torturing you, Sam," Gage teased. "The bottom line is that I want you to join me at Midgard as my executive assistant. Don has done a fantastic job, but he is taking over as my Phase III chief of operations. I need someone I can trust to manage my public and confidential activities, coordinate my staff, and help me bring Capsule fully into Phase III. If you do well, you'll have the chance to help me run the whole operation someday, and I know that you, more than any of your peers, understand why that offer is so lucrative."

Sam nodded slowly. "Yes, sir. The offer is attractive for many reasons." He considered Gage's posture with narrowed eyes. "Does my mother know—you know—about your plans for me?"

Gage sighed. "That I do not know for sure, but I will give you permission to discuss it with her if you like. She's bound to find out regardless."

True, Sam thought, but the undertones of the conversation felt ominous.

"At any rate," Gage said as he stood, "I have many other things to take care of here, including that little incident in the auditorium."

"You mean the acoustic weapon? I wouldn't worry too much; the damage was likely localized to the stage area given its amplitude."

Don returned with Sam's wristlet and the scarred man in tow, and Gage whispered something to him before turning back to Sam.

"Very good, Sam," Gage said, and his eyes pierced Sam's like knives. "You may be too quick for your own good."

Don turned to observe Sam, and Sam noticed how black his eyes were—as if he had Native American heritage.

Gage put a firm hand on Sam's shoulder. "Regardless of what you decide, you're my top pick. I know you have a tough choice between joining me or working with your mother, and I hope we will cross paths regardless." He stepped back and turned toward his assistant. "Don, please see this young man home." He winked at Sam. "Only the best for my current and future lieutenants."

He gave Sam a reassuring smile and left with his security detail. And Sam, whose mind churned with all of the unknowns, innuendo, and Gage's stunning offer, mechanically followed Don back into the corridor.

CHAPTER TEN:

THE NOTE

Don lowered the sleek, angular Falconet aircraft onto the road nearest Sam's residence. "Here we are, Mr. Richmond," he said as he powered down the engines.

"Thanks for the ride," Sam said. He flipped over the projective hood of his suit and prepared to seal it but stopped when Don called after him.

"Hey, Richmond—before I forget, do you have a pilot's license?"

"No, I don't. Only the students who wanted to be in the security forces could get into those classes."

"Oh." Don frowned. "I guess a lot has changed in the last ten years. If you decide to join our team, you'll need one. We have some superb pilots on staff who can train you."

"Okay," Sam said, distracted. *A pilot's license?* They were hard to come by, and it was yet another unexpected gift—or, given his mediocre hand-to-eye coordination—curse, in the course of a chaotic day.

Don looked at Sam out of the corner of his eye while he pulled the lever to let Sam out. "You are going to accept Dr. Gage's offer. Right?"

"It is going to be a tough decision," Sam said neutrally.

"Well, let me know either way. It was nice meeting you, Sam Richmond." Don moved a lever, and the hatch flipped open.

"Thanks, and same to you." Sam sealed his suit and watched the transport maneuver back toward the stadium in an elegant arc. When he could no longer see it, he turned back toward the rows of houses and walked between them until he arrived at his bungalow.

The hiss of the airlock and filtration system was welcome after being out in the scummy air. "Hey, Mom, I'm back," he called.

His own voice echoed back at him in reply. He checked the cloakroom again to confirm the presence of his mother's protective suit and saw it on its usual hook. *Maybe she has her headset on and can't hear me.*

"Mom?" he asked again before he checked his wristlet. *Damn.* The device was still processing whatever security protocols the Midgard team had put on it. He was about to put his suit on to walk to the Ashrafs' residence when an unusual object caught his eye.

Propped against the utensil cabinet in the galley was something white and unfamiliar. Sam moved closer to investigate and discovered that it was a piece of paper—actual paper—folded over with his name written on the front edge. Sam had seen that handwriting on some of Miranda's old lab notes. The paper crackled with age as he picked it up and no wonder. Paper was a rare and cost-prohibitive commodity these days, and this piece was edged with a thick, silver gilt finish.

The note was written with real ink, too, and it looked—and smelled—fresh. His eyes were immediately drawn to his mother's signature at the bottom—just "Miranda" with flourishes at the beginning and end. The word "Mom" was in parentheses next to it. *Strange.* The contents were stranger still:

My darling Sam,

By now you will have realized that I am not at home. I've left and I will not return, and I implore you not to waste any unnecessary time in a futile effort to find me.
You are capable of great things, and I, or, rather, my legacy, would likely prove to be an impediment instead of an asset. I know without me around, you will make the right decisions for your career, your future, and the futures of those you care about.
Be strong, be bold, and know that I carry you with me.

Love,
Miranda (Mom)

Sam slumped at the galley island where, only a few hours before, he had eaten breakfast with her. He read and re-read the letter, hoping the words would absorb the disbelief that, despite his best efforts, crept over him in a slow, steady swell. *She is gone.* He felt empty, hollow as he sat there, the note laid out on the table before him.

The pendant had been her farewell gift, not a good luck trinket. He pulled it out of his pocket. The broken chain was now a poignant analogy—proof of Miranda's departure. He felt grief and resentment rising from within. *Why? Why would she leave like this?*

As if in answer, his wristlet initialized and buzzed with all of the messages he'd missed. He flipped through them dully. Most were from Tamara. Sam flipped to the last message, which was from Don. It read:

Dr. Gage eagerly awaits your reply and asks that you give his best to Dr. Richmond.

The message, so simple on the surface, both severed Sam from his past and beckoned him toward his new future.

PART II

Lies go down easier when you want them to be true.

—JOHN OLIVER.

CHAPTER ELEVEN:

ENNUI

Midgard Capsule, May 2155

So, Sam thought as he looked around Midgard's conference room, *this is my life. What a disappointment.*

He sat in his usual position at Dr. Gage's left. Gage himself was at the head of the long, rectangular table that nearly filled the space, and Don Anianwi, now Capsule's chief of staff, sat on Gage's right. The rest of Midgard's senior leaders and administrators sat in various positions according to their seniority and rank. Their eyes were fixed on a three-dimensional digital image of a Phase III capsule while its director, Alicia Gallant, droned on about the havoc a series of hurricanes had wreaked on her domain. As she spoke, the figure of the capsule glowed red to emphasize the location of the damage and its impact.

"The rainfall levels were unprecedented," she said, "and our desalinization tanks short-circuited. Unfortunately, our water replicators were unable to compensate. They cannot handle that kind of volume on their own. We've had to reduce our water rations to tide us over until emergency replenishment arrives."

I'll bet she didn't even realize that was a pun. Sam repressed a grin as that irreverent thought crossed his mind, and he wondered how many of the remote participants were actually paying attention. Unlike those present in the room, they were not under the close scrutiny of Stephan Gage or his lieutenants. He looked up and, sure enough, the holograms of faces that hung over the capsule display like ghosts had the deadened, hollow look of phantoms. *Small wonder,* he mused. Like most of the Capsule staff, they were beaten down by a constant cycle of problems and problem-solving to the point that they were inured from anyone else's pain.

On occasion, someone with similar challenges—flooding in this case—would offer advice or ask questions, but even those interruptions were rare. *How can we—how can I—be working on something so important and feel so... so unaffected?*

With astonishment, Sam realized he was bored. Despite the mental and physical demands of Midgard's day-to-day activities—and the constant reminders that it was one of the only viable defenses against the demise of humankind, capsule life was predictable in terms of the volume of challenges that poured in, if not the type. The rest was an existence of perpetual monotony encased in large, transparent domes. *Buried alive,* Sam realized with an inward shudder. *We all agreed to be buried alive.*

He was pulled from this reverie by the irritated pitch of Dr. Gage's voice. "Look, Alicia, you've given all of us a painfully detailed explanation of what went wrong and your interim workarounds, which is useful to an extent. However, I'm more interested in how you and your team plan to fix the problems you've identified in the long term."

Sam imagined that Alicia, one of the more capable capsule directors, would have blushed visibly if the hologram program allowed. "We're working on a plan right now, sir. It will be ready for review before your scheduled battlefield circulation next month."

Dr. Gage nodded but pressed his lips together. *He's frustrated,* Sam thought, surprised. One of Gage's strongest traits as a leader was his ability to remain upbeat or, at worst, impassive in the face of continual disappointments.

"Very well. But I need to know sooner rather than later if we need to decommission the Augusta capsule. We can use its resources elsewhere, but we must initiate the transition before total failure."

Alicia looked deflated, as if what little energy reserves she had just collapsed. Those present in the room, however, sat up, their interest piqued. The decision to decommission a capsule was an exceptional occurrence, and one Dr. Gage would not use as an idle threat. Everyone knew that each failed capsule doomed thousands more people to an early demise. But keeping a dwindling capsule afloat weakened those that were functional. "It's risky either way," Dr. Gage had admitted to Sam and Don in private, "but I will not allow sunk costs to drown our entire operation."

Sam scrutinized his mentor. *This is not a sudden decision. He's probably thought about closing Augusta down for some time.* And knowing Dr. Gage, he might well have already made his final determination. Four of the Phase II capsules and two of the Phase III capsules had been decommissioned since the program's inception. After he went through the documentation and other materials associated with those efforts, Sam concluded that the Capsule program, like other Human Resiliency efforts, was trying to do too much too fast, and with too little appreciation for the exponential deterioration of the environment.

Wait—the environment. That was the missing element. Sam started in his seat, raised his eyebrows at Dr. Gage and, after he received a nod of approval, moved to the terminal at the end of the conference room. He palmed in and immediately pulled the records of all active and inactive capsules in or near flood plains. His fingers moved through flood mitigation projects and capsule schematics with the fluidity of someone who was playing a musical instrument.

Out of the corner of his eye, he noticed Rob Michaud, Capsule's chief engineer, nudge his neighbor with an indulgent smile. The senior staff was accustomed to Sam's exploits, and they waited for his magic touch to yield its golden insights. He tried not to take obvious notice, though, as he was conscious of the need to keep himself in his place lest he unintentionally threaten the competitive, type-A personalities of his colleagues.

"Thanks, Alicia," Dr. Gage said in response to some of her additional thoughts. His eyes glittered like pebbles under water as he looked over the heads of his staff. "Sam, what do you have for us?"

Sam tapped in a code for the digital display, and the image of the capsule shifted until the maze of subterranean corridors that housed the power and water production systems was visible. "You're right, sir, we need to decommission Augusta, but we can salvage most of its functions within a month or two."

Those present sat—or hovered—in stunned silence. A few glanced nervously at each other. Dr. Gage cleared his throat and said, "Okay, Sam. Please explain."

Sam was careful to maintain a neutral tone, as if what he discussed was common knowledge. "The short-circuit in Director Gallant's desalinization tanks was, as she said, caused by flooding, but the tank failure was the result of a larger issue." Sam tapped the terminal display, and the foundation walls and base of the Augusta capsule turned red.

Blue arrows simulated the flow of water against the structure, which slowly disintegrated.

"The pH levels in the water are fluctuating far more rapidly than our models predicted," he continued, "and the concrete used for Phase III construction is, as we know, inferior due to the poor quality of sand available. As the acidity in the water breaks down the concrete, it becomes more porous, which, even in dry weather, allows carbon dioxide in the atmosphere to cause further damage." Sam looked from the model to Dr. Gage. "The desalinization tanks were likely already compromised by the time the short-circuit occurred, and my guess is that the other compartments will fail successively over the next six months."

Gage rested his chin on his clasped hands while he watched the simulated structural collapse of another of his Phase III capsules. "I'm not sure there will be much left to salvage, Sam," he said, grimly.

"I'm getting to that, sir." He manipulated the screen so that another, smaller capsule appeared. "As you know, the old Columbia Capsule, which was shut down two years ago, is less than a hundred kilometers from the Augusta Capsule. Not only is it not located in a floodplain, but its underground infrastructure was also built with high-quality reinforced concrete. Its sustainment capacity is smaller than Augusta's, but their team could salvage their operations at the Columbia site until a more suitable location for a new Phase III capsule elsewhere in the region is found."

Dr. Gage cracked a smile. "An interesting notion, Sam." He pondered the idea for a moment and watched the heads around the room alternately shake and nod as others digested the information.

"Nice work, Sam." Robert Michaud leaned over and winked, and his wrinkles deepened with satisfaction. "Our decommissioned Phase II capsules are a good fallback option. It will take some work but," he turned to Dr. Gage, "I think it is worth trying. Far better than parceling Augusta's resources across other capsules that may not be prepared to receive them."

Alicia Gallant's face lit up for the first time that day, and Sam could have sworn he saw her holographic image glow. "Yes, we could make that happen in less than a month with some additional ground and aerial transport assets. The only issue is that we will have nearly five-hundred personnel over Columbia's capacity."

"That is an asset, not a problem," Dr. Gage interjected. "Our whole program will benefit from distributing experienced Phase III workers to the rest of the team." He stood up, which meant he had transitioned from listening mode to Director mode, and the rest of his staff did likewise.

"Include our human capital management team in your planning call and be prepared to give me an update in the next seventy-two hours." His eyes circled the faces around the room until they rested on Sam. "I hope you all see the benefit of having an outside eye looking at inside problems. Keep that lesson in mind for the future. We will reconvene our regional reviews tomorrow morning at the same time. You are dismissed."

The staff stood to attention briefly and exited in a flood of charcoal and other dark colors. Don clasped Sam's shoulder before he joined the crowd and shut the door. One by one the overhead holograms disappeared. Alicia's was the last, and she mouthed a "thank you" to Sam before her image dissolved.

Dr. Gage faced Sam with his hands on his hips, but he smiled. "Nice work. You made that look easy, Sam. I'd love to spend a day inside your head, though I'd probably be exhausted at the end of it."

"Just another day at Midgard, sir." Sam held his shoulders tight to prevent a dismissive shrug.

Unfortunately, the movement did not go unnoticed. "Obviously, we are not stretching you enough," Gage said with a wry smile. "Except, of course, with your flying lessons."

Sam felt his face warm. "Jody is doing her best, sir. The problem is me."

"I'm well aware of that, Sam, though I appreciate your candor. I believe your piloting abilities will eventually be passable, if not quite to the level of Ms. Escobar's." He sat down and invited Sam to join him. "I've been toying with the idea of expanding the scope of your responsibilities. It was always my plan to do so, but you've already mastered in months what I expected you to do in years. In short, you're ahead of schedule."

Sam did not know what to say. His achievements, so impressive to others, always felt normal to him. "Uh, thanks, sir. What did you have in mind?"

"I'd like to send you to a special unit for a six-month rotation. Working with them will give you the opportunity to acquire some additional skillsets and extend your analytical powers." His eyes narrowed. "We need to round you out if you're to become invincible."

Sam's reply was automatic. "No one is invincible, sir."

Dr. Gage raised his eyes to the ceiling. "Always the literal one. I know, Sam. What I was trying to communicate without insulting you is that your superior brain cannot compensate for your lack of ah—operational experience."

The flush in Sam's cheeks deepened. As he had discovered during his first few weeks at Midgard, the capsules were protected labs, insulated from the privations of the world outside. He had indeed longed for a fuller experience, but Dr. Gage had insisted on swaddling him. "When do you want me to leave, sir?"

Dr. Gage gave a short laugh. "Don't look so excited about leaving me yet, Sam. I want you around here for a few more months at least. Plus, I know you want to spend time with your friends from Phoenix during their tour here."

Sam thought for a moment and then nodded. "Yes, sir. You're right." The Phoenix capsule where Hector and Tamara were stationed was, in contrast to Augusta, a sterling example of a successful enterprise. They were sending a group of experts to Midgard that week, and Sam had volunteered to organize the excursion.

"In fact," Gage added as he stood and made for the door, "I want you to free up an afternoon during the Phoenix visit. You have few friends here, and I understand why, but I worry that you have too much time with your own thoughts, in your own head. You need to socialize more and integrate more on a personal level. Start thinking and acting like you live here and will spend the rest of your life here."

Gage's comments dismayed Sam on more than one level. It was true that he had struggled with interpersonal relationships, and the reminder about being stuck in a capsule for the rest of his existence depressed him further.

"You're right, sir. I need to try harder. And I appreciate the time with my friends."

Gage stopped with his hand on the handle and turned back toward Sam. "You're welcome, and good luck with Ms. Ashraf. She'd be a fool to turn you down. Oh, and try not to kill yourself training with Ms. Escobar tomorrow. I'd hate to be the one to have to tell your friends that they lost you to your own ineptitude."

Trust Dr. Gage to raise my spirits and dash them in the same sentence. "Yes, sir. I'll let you know how it goes with Tam—I mean Ms. Ashraf."

"As you should. I'm the one who has to sign off on her transfer and joint accommodations here after all." He grinned and walked out the door as Sam followed, lost in thought.

CHAPTER TWELVE:

THE FLAGSHIP

"Turn now. Now!"

Sam recognized the panic masquerading as urgency in the pitch of Jody Escobar's voice."Copy," he replied and steered toward their new course. A dark shape loomed in his path.

"No!" Jody yelled. "Up and right, up and right. Damn it, Richmond!" The Falconet cruiser veered so sharply that it went almost perpendicular to the ground. As it ascended, it narrowly avoided contact with a mountainside hidden in the early morning haze.

"Okay, flatten her out a bit."

Sam struggled with the controls and felt perspiration moisten his hands.

"Any time now, Richmond, any ti—shit! Pull out! Pull out!" Jody yanked on her yoke as the craft shook with the force of the turn.

"I've got it!" he protested. "I've goottttt iiiitttt..."

The landscape closed on the periphery of his vision as if he were in a trash compactor. The shapes around him blurred, and his head pulsed with pain. He blinked hard and exhaled to stave off unconsciousness, but the fuzzy images dimmed into blackness.

In a rush, fluorescent light replaced the darkness, and Sam found himself back in the room from his dream. The faceless man in black again stood next to him, and the unknown voice beckoned him to choose.

But before Sam could answer, the mysterious man spoke. "No. He is with me. With us." The man was insistent, and Sam felt himself being dragged away. Instead of putting him in a headlock this time, however, the man pinned Sam's arms while a bag was thrown over his head, smothering him. As he struggled to breathe, the fluorescent lights flickered. He heard a woman's voice in the background but could not understand her over the roaring in his ears.

"Richmond. Richmond! Sam! Snap out of it."

Sam groaned and blinked his eyes. Jody hovered over him, her amber eyes full of concern. He saw her face begin to swirl. "Hey," he said weakly, "I think I'm gonna—" He retched before he finished his sentence.

"Oh, no, you don't, Richmond, not on me," Jody admonished as she rolled him onto his side. "Feel free to spill your guts now."

Sam's body complied with the command even as his mind rebelled. When his stomach finally ceased its spasms, he pushed himself up on one elbow. "How long was I out?"

Jody eyed him warily, still suspicious that something might actually be left in his stomach. "About five minutes. I was worried when you didn't wake up once we leveled off, so I performed an emergency landing at the surveyors' encampment. They've docked us in their hangar and helped me haul you out. I'd have called the medics if you'd been down much longer."

She smiled, but Sam saw the tension in her jaw, and her burnished skin was pale. *She was more worried than she is letting on.* "Yeah, sorry about that."

"Don't apologize." She sighed and sat back on her heels as Sam moved gingerly to a sitting position. "It was my mistake. I knew you weren't ready to fly on pure instrument control yet, but—"

"But I made you do it anyway," he finished.

"Weeelll, that and Dr. Gage basically ordered me to give you more airtime in crummy conditions. He said you needed practice." She stood up and held out her hand. "He wasn't joking."

Sam took the proffered hand and tested his ability to stand. Although his legs shook slightly, his balance was restored. "Seriously," he said as he observed a friction burn on the Falconet's side, "I'll train as much he wants me to, but he should just accept the fact that he needs a real professional at the helm, particularly with the constant weather shifts."

Jody tried to lighten the mood. "You know, there is no time like the present to learn to trust the aircraft's computers. They know what they're doing."

He pointed to his head. "Yes, intellectually, I know that is true. However, I hate turning over decisions to an inanimate system."

"And I hate performing emergency transfers when you pull enough Gs to knock yourself out. How else do you expect to manage the conditions you fly in, idiot? You lost your orientation pretty quickly in that soup out there, and that is what the technology is for—to help you get it back."

Her hands were on her hips, and Sam held out his palms in mock supplication. "You're right. I am an idiot, and experience is a harsh teacher."

A grumble of frustration rumbled in Jody's throat. "Not harsh enough, apparently. Let me put this another way." She moved toward him and clamped her hands down on his shoulders. "Samuel Richmond, you are not allowed to kill yourself or otherwise die on my watch unless I personally decide to kill you, which I very well may if you don't start internalizing some of those lessons."

Sam forced himself not to back away. "Yes, Ms. Escobar." His lips twitched.

"Ugh. I might have to kill you anyway if you ever call me that again." She shoved him back in pretend disgust and clambered up the ladder. "Anyhow, don't you have a meeting to go to or something?"

Sam convulsively checked his wristlet. It was seven minutes past five. "Crap. Yes, I do." He stepped on the ladder and gripped tightly to accommodate his shaky legs but, to his surprise, they had stilled. He felt fine—almost normal in fact. He quirked his lips and looked at Jody, who shrugged innocently.

"The surveyors' clinic was open, so I helped myself to some stimulant serum. And I took the liberty of injecting some into your skinny little tush."

In one fluid motion, she grabbed the top of the hatch and slid her long, lithe body easily into the pilot's seat.

She moves like Hector. In fact, he reflected, the two of them had a lot in common, which was probably why he liked her so much. *I should introduce them.* Although Jody was at least five years older than Hector, he doubted the age gap would matter, and the thought of linking Hector romantically with the closest thing he had to a friend at Midgard made him smile. "Thanks, Jody. You always have my back or, in this case, my bottom."

"You know it!" She grabbed his hand and helped him into the copilot's seat. "All right, let's get back to base. Strap in and keep your hands away from my controls."

"Yes, Ms.—I mean Jody," he stammered as she rallied her free hand for a playful punch. "But I will watch and pay careful attention."

She rolled her eyes as she pulled the controller with one hand and pressed a series of buttons with the other. The docking clamps released, and the Falconet hovered off the hangar floor with a gentle hum.

"You're lucky. The survey team asked me to haul back some samples, so this stop wasn't a total loss." She grinned at him as she maneuvered the agile craft through the space left by the hangar's open door and slowly ascended.

Between the surveyors' outpost and Midgard lay miles of off-limits territory known as the restricted zone. Every capsule had one for its own protection—to keep potential rogue actors and dissidents from disrupting operations. Much of the morning's fog had lifted, and Sam caught glimpses of the dead forests and rocky outcrops of the mountains to the west—the ones he had almost run into. He sighed as he observed the depressing landscape of barren hills, dead trees, and ruined hamlets.

In the distance, Midgard's transparent dome gleamed with the iridescence of a soap bubble. It was surrounded by concentric barriers of layered ground defenses that resembled the central keep of a fortified castle complex. When Sam had first seen Midgard, he had marveled at her perfection and how she emerged from the ugly, inhospitable surroundings like a beacon of hope. Now it was her imperfections that caught his attention because he knew how much even the slightest defect could disrupt—and perhaps destroy—its fragile ecosystem.

"Hmmmm," he said, more to himself than Jody, as the Falconet descended, "that solar capture station on the south side has some sort of muck on it—probably from that last acid rainstorm."

"I'm glad that's your problem and not mine," she remarked and steered toward one of Midgard's docking stations. "I've got plenty of other stuff on my plate today, like that Phoenix transport inspection." She brought the craft into the clamps in a single movement that emphasized her expert handling skills.

"Right," Sam agreed as a thrill of anticipation surged through him. "Which reminds me, I need to verify their arrival time given those tornado warnings."

"Here's hoping that they're delayed!" Jody grinned at Sam and launched herself onto the ramp. "Means I can catch up on my fitness requirement for the day."

"Good luck with that. I'm still trying to find time for mine," he responded while he checked the day's schedule on his wristlet.

A harsh beeping sound interrupted his efforts. *Damn!* He had worked through the evening meal last night, had skipped breakfast for his pilot lesson this morning, and now his iron and blood levels were dangerously low. *No wonder I passed out in the cockpit.*

He felt himself warm as Jody looked between his wristlet and face with one eyebrow raised. "I know, I know. I need to eat something."

"Yeah, and you may want to spruce up a bit before going to Dr. Gage's office. You still look pretty green around the gills."

"You're probably right, but I'm short on time." He attempted to smooth his hair with his hands and dust off his charcoal utility suit. He noticed that Jody, too, looked somewhat worse for wear, and her short, prematurely graying hair clustered around her ears like stalks of dead corn.

She shrugged and scratched the back of her hand. "It's your funeral. I'll take these samples down to the environmental lab, then." She waited for him to respond and, when he did not, gave him her most exasperated sigh. "You're welcome, Sam. See you tomorrow."

"Thanks!" he said as looked up from his schedule, but she was already out of earshot.

He jogged to the ramp that led toward the billeting area, passed through the interior airlock, and turned into the hallway where his room was located. The console outside glowed green when he palmed into it, and the door slid open. His furniture consisted of a twin bunk with a tiny desk underneath, a small storage compartment, and a washroom combo tucked into the far corner.

As the assistant to Dr. Gage and keeper of many secrets, Sam had better quarters than most. Private rooms were a luxury; most of Midgard's twelve hundred inhabitants bunked in narrow, windowless barracks with communal toilets and washing facilities. Many of his peers envied him the privilege, but Sam knew few would willingly change places with him if they had any inkling of the pressure and responsibilities that shadowed him like a hovering cloud.

A glimpse of his face in the mirror as he rinsed off caused him to swear. *Jody was right.* The perpetual dark smudges under his eyes were enormous, and his olive complexion was pasty, almost yellow. He groomed himself as best he could, grabbed his tablet and an extra ration bar from the desk, and left for work.

Midgard's circular main corridor was on the outer ring of the dome. Sam moved from a walk to a jog as he made his way to the headquarters area, hoping his wristlet's fitness monitor would count the few minutes it took him to get there as part of his daily exercise quota. He passed a few people in subdued colors that corresponded to their capsule specialty or assignment: black for security, indigo for logistics and maintenance personnel, dull green for those growing plants and sustenance, taupe for those working in waste recycling and so on. Given the hour, the night shift's staff were prepared to transition with their counterparts as part of Midgard's twenty-four-hour operations, so more people were present than usual.

Sam knew most of them from the rotations Don had put him on during his first few months at Midgard. He had spent time with every section at the flagship to learn what their mission was and their vital role in keeping both their own station and the others across the Capsule Program operational. Dr. Gage expected Sam to be able to jump in with any team or group at any time and convey the Director's vision, intent, and instructions in his absence. Consequently, although Sam was well-liked, professional distance sequestered him from any close personal relationships.

Those people he encountered in the hallway either nodded or hailed him as he passed but made no effort to start a conversation. A few smiled and shook their heads when Sam's wristlet beeped at him to eat again, and Sam blushed. He slowed to a walk before the door to the leadership suite and wiped his sweat-dampened hand on his trousers before he placed it on the scanner. It warmed beneath his palm and turned from red to yellow to green. The door slid open, and Sam was greeted by a brisk, cheerful voice.

"Good morning, Sam! Hey, I have a quick question for you. It's—geez, what happened to you?"

"Flying lesson," Sam said tersely. "Good morning to you, too, Rayna."

The corners of Rayna's mouth curved up. "And here I was hoping that you'd start the day off on a positive note for a change." Dr. Gage's staff manager, Rayna Martinez, had a contagious, cheerful aura, and Sam both liked and valued her competence and discretion. Somewhere in her early thirties, she guarded her boss from unwelcome visitors and requests more viciously than Canadian coywolves guarded their hard-won meals.

"Are you all set for today?" She munched on a nutrient bar with one hand as she fingered through her terminal with the other.

"Almost," he responded and sat down at his desk opposite hers. "I need to verify the Phoenix transport's arrival time and reschedule the Southeast Region planning session."

"Ummmm," she said, her mouth full. She held up her hand to alert him to the news she wanted to impart. "I just got the word from Southwest. Their transport is on a two-hour delay."

Sam swore, and Rayna raised her eyebrows. The throbbing pain in his head intensified while he mentally tabulated all the favors he would have to call in to assuage the grumpy, overworked security and logistics personnel with yet another change to the schedule. And, if that weren't enough, his wristlet beeped its alarm again.

Rayna narrowed her eyes. "You forgot to eat again. Didn't you? You need to get something in your stomach before you face the day."

"Thanks, Rayna, I was getting to that." He waved his bar at her. "See?"

Before he could even break it out of its container, however, Dr. Gage barged into the outer office.

"Sam, set up the secure communications link immediately. We have a serious situation on our hands."

CHAPTER THIRTEEN:

THE GENERAL

Stephan Gage's face was taut with suppressed fury. "Well, don't just sit there," he growled to a dumbstruck Sam. "Move out!"

Sam jumped to his feet. "Which channel, sir?"

"Seventeen." He waved Sam away and leaned over to instruct an equally unsettled Rayna.

The hairs on the back of Sam's neck raised, and he hastened into his boss's private office.

Seventeen. It was the most protected communications frequency and Gage's direct line to one very specific person.

He palmed into the terminal at the desk and primed the optic netting. At the center of the office was a table covered with a terrain model of all fifty-seven capsules, and Sam moved it to one side. Satisfied with the setup, he mechanically organized and synchronized the codes and shapes on the screen into the highest security pattern while his mind ran through the possible scenarios that could have caused such consternation.

Was it another major capsule failure? A government downgrade in priorities? Or the loss of a vital shipment of supplies? All were possibilities, but the first was manageable, the second was improbable, and the third was unlikely to raise the Director's blood pressure by any significant margin.

Whatever it was had severely rattled Dr. Gage, and Sam suspected his days of tedium were numbered.

"Channel seventeen open and cleared for use." The melodic tones of the computer's voice contrasted with the static that emanated from the optic netting. Within seconds, a full-body hologram of a man dressed in a black and gray camouflage uniform emblazoned with golden stars on its shoulders emerged. It blinked at him, and Sam suppressed the urge to crouch into a defensive position.

Despite the fact that he had known of Police General Anton Gage's existence for several months, he still felt like he was seeing double whenever he was in the presence of Dr. Gage's twin brother. Both men were tall and wiry, and they shared similar cropped graying hair, facial features, and keen powers of observation. Upon closer inspection, Anton's eyes had stony gray overtones that made them less translucent than Stephan's clear blue. He was also more muscular, and his face lacked the lines of humor that flanked his brother's cheeks. Even in hologram form, the General had a commanding presence and bearing that unnerved Sam like no one else.

The fact that Dr. Gage had a brother at all was extraordinary. Very few of his or succeeding generations had siblings due to the government's restrictive reproductive laws. Even natural twins like the Gages were prohibited, and Sam and a handful of others who knew of Anton's existence wondered about the circumstances that precipitated this rare exception.

"Where is my brother?" General Gage's tone was as repellent as Stephan's was inviting.

"I'm right here, Anton," Stephan Gage responded impatiently as he shut the door. "And I just arranged for our critical staff to meet later this morning. Haskill is on his way."

"I see," the General said. He crossed his arms and glared at Sam. "Why is he still here?"

Sam, who simultaneously had the same thought, stepped toward the door but stopped when he felt Dr. Gage's hand on his shoulder.

"Sam stays," he said firmly.

General Gage raised his eyebrows. "Oh? Mr. Richmond has not been indoctrinated yet."

"He will be and, under the circumstances, the sooner the better." When Anton's expression did not change, Stephan clenched his jaw. "We've discussed this, Anton. And, as you know, it is my decision, not yours."

Anton's eyes narrowed to slits. "Yes, but we agreed on certain... conditions."

Stephan waved dismissively. "Indoctrination was not one of them. I will be Mr. Richmond's guarantor until his induction."

Sam was mystified. The opportunity to join a special unit was one thing, but the notion of an indoctrination sounded ominous. *And, if General Gage has any say in the matter, it will not be pleasant.*

"As you will," Anton replied, but he might as well have said, "I wash my hands of you."

"Good, it is settled then." Stephan sat at the table and motioned for Sam to do the same. Sam did so but warmed under the heat of the General's holographic gaze. "Now, Anton, why don't you tell me everything you know about Hugo Delecroix's whereabouts?"

Sam's head jerked upward. Hugo Delecroix led the capsule near Bangor, Maine, and it was the most successful Phase II station outside of Midgard itself. Sam had met Hugo a few months previously during one of Dr. Gage's regional site visits, and he was impressed by Hugo's depth of knowledge, his willingness to acknowledge mistakes, and his team's ability to recover from them. In fact, Delecroix's team was so tight that it resembled more of a family, unlike the fractious, competitive atmosphere in the rest of the Capsule program.

Anton's recitation was cold and clinical. "Delecroix failed to appear for a scheduled soil conservation review this morning. The Bangor team conducted a thorough search of the grounds and aircraft. They found no sign of him, and all transport craft are accounted for. I alerted my regional security staff, and they are on station conducting similar investigations."

"Were there any signs of foul play or any indications that he intended to leave?" Stephan Gage tried to keep his voice level.

"My people are going through his archives and personal effects and interviewing those close to him now. So far, we've discovered that John Ringner, his deputy, thought Delacroix seemed more stressed and distracted than usual but attributed it to some of the difficulties they had after last week's acid rain episode." The General pulled out a tablet and tapped onto its screen. "But our steganography decoder unearthed this image from one of his private messages."

A three-dimensional image of a red-gold maple leaf encased in a clear dome appeared on the table in front of Stephan Gage, who clenched his fists. "No," he whispered. "Hugo would not—could not do that to me. To all of us."

The General gestured to the object. "The evidence suggests otherwise. A trace check verified the source of the message it was embedded within as Montreal."

Sam was curious. *What does Canada's Capsule program have to do with any of this?* Like the United States, Canada supported several Human Resiliency initiatives, but relations between the two countries were tepid, and the sporadic collaborative efforts between them were little more than superficial.

"Face it," the General said harshly, "your elite, loyal capsule leader is a defector at best or a Canadian spy at worst, and if you don't start—" he stopped when a movement from Sam reminded him someone else was in the room, "start taking some of the special measures I recommended, others will follow. We can't afford to lose the slim margin of advantage we do have. We are on the brink of—"

"Enough!" Stephan jumped to his feet. "I have heard all I need to hear about what has happened or what might happen as a consequence of my supposed failure to implement your advice. What I am interested in is how you intend to do your job and find Hugo and our other alleged defectors."

The General, too, got to his feet, and the two brothers glowered at each other. Sam wondered whether the altercation would have turned physical had the confrontation taken place in person. Unconsciously, he set one foot behind the other and his hands at his sides for balance. He turned his head toward Dr. Gage and caught his eye. "What is it, Sam?"

"Sir, were there any disturbances in the vicinity of the Bangor capsule or its restricted area during the timeframe in which Mr. Delacroix went missing?"

The brothers stared at Sam, but the General was the first to speak. "How is that relevant?" he demanded.

"It is possible that Mr. Delecroix is neither a defector nor a spy." He swallowed and struggled to keep his voice neutral. "Depending on the circumstances, he may have disappeared."

"How do you figure?" the General asked, his face like stone.

Sam squared his shoulders. "I've been studying the disappearances ever since my—" he inhaled, controlled an unwelcome quaver, and continued, "ever since my mother left. I observed a pattern. Every high-profile disappearance has coincided with an attack or demonstration or similar occurrence, and I suspect those events were carefully crafted distractions."

To his shame, Sam's eyes moistened with the repressed memories of those first terrible days and weeks after his mother's abandonment. Although Tamara and her father had done their best to comfort him, he had been devastated, to the point where he nearly sabotaged his future prospects by making plans to go off and find Miranda on his own. Only when Hector appeared on his doorstep—and spelled out the futility of that idea in kind but firm terms—didSam stop to consider the futility of that course of action. Instead, he received permission from Dr. Gage to report for duty a month late in order to work with the investigative forces trying to locate his mother.

Unfortunately, none of the Human Resiliency, municipal, or interior investigative forces had been able to find any trace of her. Miranda's file—like so many others—was regulated to the growing stack of the Disappeared to stagnate and fade away. But Sam refused to give up and used what little spare time he had to continue his own private investigation.

"I did not realize you had studied the disappearances so closely, Sam," Stephan said as he watched Sam's face.

Sam shrugged. "It is a personal project, sir, not relevant to my duties at Midgard."

"Perhaps that was true five minutes ago, but is no longer," Stephan mused more to himself than to Sam. He returned his attention to his brother. "Do you see now why I wanted him?"

"Hmmph," grunted the General. "Maybe. Though I reserve judgment until my people are able to explore this theory."

"Well, why don't you start by answering Sam's question, Anton, and we can go from there."

The General looked at Sam as if he would rather shoot him than admit his oversight. "Yes, Richmond, there was a—an event in the vicinity, but you won't hear about it in the news because it took place within the Maine capsule's restricted zone."

Stephan Gage raised an eyebrow. "Oh? When were you going to tell me about that incident, Anton?"

"Eventually," the General responded crisply. "You would have seen it in the serious incident report roll-up for the week. And, no, I am not going to share the details with you in front of an unindoctrinated person. That is my call, if you remember."

"Fine," Stephan acknowledged. "We can discuss the specifics later. I look forward to seeing what your analysts make of Sam's assessment."

The General made a noncommittal gesture. "Yes, we will see. And now I must participate in one of the interviews."

"Fine. We will speak later. Midgard One out." Dr. Gage punctuated his words with a vicious tap on his tablet that ended the call. He sat down, rested his chin in his hands, and looked, unseeing, at the diorama on the table. Sam waited for dismissal. When it did not come, he moved toward the door but was stopped by the sound of Dr. Gage's voice.

"Sam, how soon do you think you can be ready to leave for that special assignment we discussed?"

A quickening heartbeat thudded in Sam's ears. "As… as soon as the Phoenix visit is over, sir."

Dr. Gage hit himself on the forehead. "Of course. I had almost forgotten. You've got an important milestone coming up." He smiled at Sam ruefully, his eyes were tight with strain.

Sam made an involuntary movement toward the breast pocket of his uniform, which held a small, oval-shaped container. Gage saw the movement and repressed a full-blown grin. "Naturally, all of the information you just heard is classified, so please do not disclose any of that information to your friends. I expect Hugo's... departure will be common knowledge soon enough, but don't discuss it until the bulletin posts."

"I understand, sir. Speaking of which, the Phoenix transport is delayed for weather."

"Yes, I know." Dr. Gage sighed. "These delays are becoming more frequent. Frankly, I don't know why we bother with such tight schedules for the visits. Just tell Steve Haskill to give everyone a quick security brief when they disembark and then they can all have the afternoon to get settled."

"Yes, sir," he responded and turned away so the Director would not see him grimace. Haskill, the director of Midgard's security and the head of the Capsule security force, was not the most pleasant person to deal with.

"Oh, and make sure Ms. Escobar knows that she's on call for the Phoenix site visits. I'd like our guests to live long enough to tell the tale of our magnificence," Gage quipped.

Sam looked at Dr. Gage flush with embarrassment but saw that his eyes sparkled with laughter. *Clearly, this morning's escapade did not go unnoticed.* An incessant beeping noise interrupted the moment of shared camaraderie.

"And why don't you eat something before you pass out on me," Dr. Gage said as he suppressed a chuckle.

"Yes, sir, I'll do that now."

"You had better. The last thing I need is my left-hand man and secret weapon going down." He dismissed Sam with a wave of his hand as Steve Haskill entered with a grim-looking member of Midgard's intelligence cell.

CHAPTER FOURTEEN:

THE ATTACK

Tamara Ashraf, assistant harvester for the Phoenix capsule's agriculture team, pressed her cheek against the glass of the narrow, scratched window of her transport to observe the Appalachian Mountains. At least she thought it was the Appalachians. Geography and navigation had never been her strong points. The charred remnants of what had once been forests scarred and pitted the landscape, and she shivered. The sight was reminiscent of her recent failed potato crop, and it reminded her of how bleak her future would be if she could not do better.

"Hey, *corazón,* are you okay?"

Hector's deep voice rumbled pleasantly in her ear, and she turned from the window. Despite her mood, her cheeks dimpled. She loved it when Hector used terms of endearment in his native Spanish. "Yes, I'm fine. I'm just trying to forget my latest screw-up so that I don't spoil our Midgard trip."

He squeezed her hand. "I told you, you have to get over it and move on. We are all learning, and we all have to deal with things that are outside our control. It was your turn to have a bad outcome last week, and it will probably be my turn the next time."

Tamara gave an exaggerated sigh but allowed her lips to break into a full-blown smile. She knew Hector was right—as usual—but he had not struggled as she had. She wanted so badly to prove herself that she had put in a ridiculous amount of extra study and lab time, but this additional effort had not assuaged her underlying fear that the Accessions board and Miranda Richmond had made a mistake when they selected her for the Capsule program. If not the potatoes, it was the mushrooms or the kelp beds that died or broke out in some obscure blight. She could not remember the last time any of her assigned crops survived; even those that persisted in the lab failed in a live environment. After each botched effort, she analyzed the mold or spores or whatever had killed the crop but to no avail. At times, it felt like nature and fate were taunting her. She knew if she continued down that road, she was at risk of being downgraded out of the Capsule program.

"Thanks for the pep talk, Mister-I-just-got-promoted-like-ten-years-earlier-than-I-expected." Tamara meant for the words to come out lightly, but she could not conceal her frustration.

"Whoa, there. I had nothing to do with that," Hector protested. "Dr. Singh's move wasn't exactly planned, and his replacement was pulled over to Nashua at the last minute. I was the only person left to promote!"

"And you're the only guy I know who could run an entirely new fitness regimen every day of the week on four hours of sleep and still have energy left over to joke about it. Humility doesn't suit you, by the way, even if it is genuine."

He drew back. "You know, becoming the new Physical Endurance Director this soon or this way wasn't my idea."

She was immediately contrite. "I know. I know. I'm sorry. It is just hard for me to watch you do so well without even trying when I work my tail off, but I can't get anything to come out right."

"If it makes you feel better, I am buried under about a terabyte's worth of bureaucratic nonsense right now. I haven't had time to take a Falconet out for a spin in weeks." He sighed and looked at his hands, which were now folded in his lap. "I miss flying. It was my escape. This trip is the only aerial experience I've had since the big promotion and riding a Stingray would not have been my first choice."

"Poor Hector," she mocked. "Just remember, there are some benefits." She wiggled her eyebrows at him and grinned. "Like your new accommodations."

Hector's posture relaxed. "That is one benefit I am happy to take on along with my new workload." He leaned over and kissed her gently on the lips.

Tamara savored the kiss momentarily but pulled away when she caught the smirks and whispers of the passengers around her. Her nether regions tingled when she thought about that first night after Hector had moved out of the barracks and into his new private room. In addition to being incredibly attractive, Hector had skill and endurance in just about every type of physical activity as far as she could tell. It would be hard to be separated from him for most of this trip, but that was the least of her worries.

"Well, if you don't feel like hugging right now, corazón, this will have to do." As Hector spoke, he reached over and belted Tamara into her seat's harness.

"What are you doing?" She giggled. "We're out of range of all of that tornado activity by now."

"Consider it a virtual embrace," he said and stole another kiss. His eyes sparkled with mischief and, oddly, excitement. "Now we both daydream in peace and safety until we get to Midgard." He winked at her, buckled his harness, and reclined his seat.

Midgard. The word gave her butterflies, and not all of them were of the pleasant type. She still had no idea how she was going to break the news about Hector to Sam. Even though she tried to convince herself otherwise, she knew he would be devastated. *Not that it's all my fault,* she reminded herself. After Miranda's departure, Sam had been distant and preoccupied, and he was in no mood for romance. Although they had corresponded regularly since beginning their respective capsule assignments, opportunities to be around each other were rare, and she had missed him. Or, rather, she missed the old Sam—the geeky, keenly intelligent Sam whose head stayed in the clouds while his awkward body stumbled over every crack in the pavement.

But that Sam had disappeared along with Miranda and, given the weight of his responsibilities and his ambitions, he just might be gone forever. There had, however, been a brief moment when she thought her Sam might have returned. In January, she, Hector, and Sam had spent their annual vacation time together at Lake Tahoe. On their last morning there, Sam had joined her by the water while Hector had planned their return flight. Sam had looked at her with his old, crooked smile and softly brushed her hair out of her eyes. Tamara's heart leapt, and she strummed with anticipation of declaration. Instead, he received a stupid alert on his damn wristlet and the opportunity passed untaken.

Hector, on the other hand, was always around and always flirting with her and telling her how amazing she was, even when she felt the opposite. He was also persistent, adamant that he would wait for her to come around because, he confidently told her, he knew she would. That kind of assuredness annoyed her, but she was flattered that the most gorgeous guy on the station lapped at her heels when he could have had anyone else there in a heartbeat. Moreover, who wouldn't want to have a friend and confidant who was an open book and a superb listener?

Yes, Tamara marveled at all of those things about Hector except—except there was no chase, no puzzle, no challenge with him. But she had reasoned that her work was difficult enough, and she loved the woman he believed her to be. Secretly, she hoped that maybe, just maybe, she could grow into that person with a man like Hector at her side.

The gentle hum of the transport's electric engine whirred rhythmically as it accelerated, and Tamara felt herself drifting into dreams of helping a man with Hector's looks but Sam's determination and drive. Together, they would run the entire Capsule program someday, and they would shepherd their people into a new future. He would be the unquestionable leader, but she would be the secret advisor, the quiet power behind the man. She felt the weight of their child on her hip, a beautiful—

"What the hell? Everyone strap in! Now!"

The shout from the cockpit drew Tamara sharply back into the present. The Stingray banked hard to the right. She glanced out of the window as gravity forced her into Hector's shoulder, and she saw an enormous, green-black mass of cumulonimbus clouds sparkling with electricity. It loomed in front of the mountain range she had observed with disquiet earlier, and the sight caused her hands and feet to prickle with adrenaline.

Hector saw it, too. "Oh my god. Where the heck did that come from?" As the words left his lips, he braced Tamara with his solid frame. Some other passengers scrambled for their seats and fumbled with harnesses as the transport shuddered and bounced with the sudden onset of high winds.

Hector and Tamara watched in horror as the clouds rotated into a cyclone-like vortex, expanded, and swallowed one of their transport's Goshawk Interceptor escorts.

"Evasive action! Bank south, bank south!" the pilot shouted to his copilot as the craft continued to veer steeply to the right. It leveled off at speed through a nearby valley. Tamara opened her mouth to voice a question to Hector when a sudden impact to the aircraft's rear caused it to violently shudder and moan.

Tamara screamed, and her voice joined a chorus of expletives and yelling as the cabin filled with smoke and started a jerky descent. Two passengers were thrown against the bulkhead. The engine made loud, arrhythmic whomping noises as it shook viciously. The crying and yelling crescendoed and, at the same time, the pilot yelled, "Dutch! Dutch! Wake up! I need your help."

Alert to the call for assistance, Hector unfastened his harness. "Tam, I've got to go. Stay buckled in," he shouted as he reached for the emergency strap.

"No! Don't leave me! Please don't leave me!"

He saw her panic and felt her frenetic grip as his utility suit ripped with the force of her tug. He held her at arm's length, looked directly into her wide brown eyes, and mouthed, "It will be okay. I've got this." He wrested himself free.

She watched him move to the cabin with the same grace and agility he exhibited on the obstacle courses he designed. Moving hand over hand, he used the straps to maneuver down the wobbling, tilted aisle with feline nimbleness until he came across a concussed colleague. He deftly lifted the man off the floor and heaved him toward a person who was belted in and helped them secure the limp form. Then he disappeared into the cockpit.

Tamara heard him yell something to the pilot and then saw the bloodied sprawl of the copilot lowered to the floor between the seats. She looked away and tried to take deep, controlled breaths so she could remain conscious.

Another deafening boom raged as an object contacted the aircraft's starboard side. The transport, which was already pitched right, began a semi-inverted dive toward the ground as its starboard side burst into flames. Everything seemed to move in slow motion. Tamara felt herself howl out a warning to Hector but could not hear the words. She looked down at her harness and watched her hands release the buckle as she shoved herself away from the fire. The burning smell assaulted her nostrils, and her back and shoulder stung. Before she could inspect the damage, she crashed sideways into the row of seats on the opposite side of the aisle. The man she collided with cried out in alarm, but he grabbed her tightly to stop her from tumbling into the opposite bulkhead.

"Grab the extinguisher!" someone yelled, coughing. The smoke in the cabin thickened.

Extinguisher? Thought Tamara. *What is an extinguisher?* Her panicked mind reached for something concrete but was unable to link words to their meanings. She felt someone step on her, but the act did not register any pain. A loud hissing noise caught her attention, and she felt some of the heat dissipate, but the smoke and cacophony of sounds rapidly overcame her remaining senses.

The transport continued its spiraling descent as the vibrations intensified. She looked back up toward her window. The last conscious thing she registered through the fiery haze was a blackening sky.

CHAPTER FIFTEEN:

THE AFTERMATH

Sam sprinted toward the main entrance's cloakroom and donned his protective suit as fast as his trembling hands could manage. He activated its seal with one hand while he tried to enter the egress code with the other. After several attempts, the door to the docking station ramp opened, and he jogged down toward Steve Haskill and a handful of others. All of them stared upward at the sky. When Sam did likewise, his transparent face shield darkened to reflect light from the setting sun, which contrasted strangely with the menacing black and green haze of the tornado.

The alert that Dr. Gage, Sam, and the members of Midgard's crisis response team had received moments earlier stated only that the storm had appeared without triggering any advanced warning mechanisms, and that it had wreaked havoc with the delayed Stingray transport from Phoenix. As terrified as he was for Hector and Tamara's safety, Sam could not stop himself from reviewing likely scenarios that would have precipitated such an event. He concluded that the timing of both the storm and the missile attack suggested a deliberate, well-planned ambush. But he had no idea who would want to destroy a transport carrying people who were trying to save the world.

"Yes, Midgard Station is online and reads you." Haskill spoke into the receiver built into his helmet. Sam shifted his weight and wrung his hands during the short pause that followed. "Yes, yes," Haskill said in a raised voice. "We are aware of the incident and will get the details later. Tracking at least eight casualties and a downed rear thruster. We scrambled some Goshawks for additional protection, and they will arrive any minute—they've arrived? Good. No—No! Just stop talking and focus. Keep it together, kid."

Although he knew the command was not for him, Sam treated it as if it was. His brain was in overdrive, and he still felt light-headed from the jolt of the initial report. The last thing anyone needed right now was for him to be added to the casualty list. *The transport can still fly. That is a good sign,* he reminded himself. But the still faceless casualties began to assume the visages of those he knew—and loved.

Haskill issued commands to his team, and an emergency crew armed with fire retardant positioned themselves around the docking station. Sam looked again toward the horizon, and he thought he saw some mobile dark blots silhouetted by the setting sun.

"Look," someone cried and pointed at the spots, which had increased in size. "Stand by to receive," Haskill ordered. Medics arrived with stretchers and treatment equipment as one of Midgard's Goshawk Interceptors hummed overhead. Sam watched the sleek silver disc move at an angle over the glittering dome. Though small—they had a complement of up to three personnel—the Goshawks were the swiftest craft in the Capsule fleet. They were also armed with hull-penetrating lasers as well as traditional projectiles. Deadly and elegant, much like their namesake, they were typically used to deter aggressors rather than as an offensive capability. But they were no match for a tornado.

The Stingray's pilot lowered the smoking, nearly tailless transport into the dock, and it coughed into silence when it locked into place. Black smoke rose in wisps from the rear and starboard sides. Two more Goshawks hovered overhead and prepared to respond to any additional aggression.

Sam paced on the ramp while the emergency crew sprayed the aircraft with retardant until the entire thing was a foaming, frothy mess. *Please let them be okay. Let her be okay,* he whispered repeatedly while he watched helplessly.

Someone called, "Clear," and waved the crisis team forward. The Stingray's front hatch lowered, and the craft belched out an ugly gray haze along with some moaning, staggering human forms. Sam saw a pair of singed and bloody passengers stumble down the hatch onto the platform. One of them had a huge gash down their side, and another, hobbled by a leg injury, limped with some assistance. Behind them came a perspiring, smoke-stained Hector, who reached up with his free hand to wipe blood and sweat out of his eyes. Over his shoulder, he carried a clumsy bundle topped with a frizzy mop of dark hair.

"Hector? Hector! Is she all right?"

Hector turned his head toward the sound of Sam's voice for a fraction of a second and then made a beeline for the medics. With some assistance, he lowered to his knees and guided Tamara's body to a stretcher. Sam stepped closer and thought he saw her eyelids flicker and her face contort with pain. A firm grip on his shoulder prevented him from rushing to her side.

"No, Sam. Stay back and let our folks have the space they need to do their job. You can join your friends in the infirmary later." Dr. Gage's voice was tight, but Sam could hear the compassion under the veneer.

They watched in silence while the rest of the crisis team evacuated the remaining passengers and inspected the transport for additional damage. Although Sam did not care for Steve Haskill, he admired the way the man was able to coordinate bedlam into movements so synchronous that they might have been a dance.

A sudden halt from Haskell jarred the otherwise smooth transition from chaos to an orderly evacuation. Even at a distance, Sam saw the alarm on his stolid features as he waved his hands wildly. "Everyone get back inside, now! The battery is going critical!"

Dr. Gage, Sam, and Haskill's team ushered the other observers to the main airlock. The transport hissed out a rusty substance. Behind Haskill, Sam saw a familiar lithe figure in a flame-retardant suit sprint down the platform and into the mouth of the Stingray.

"Close the blast doors!" Someone pulled a lever near the entrance and the heavily shielded panels slid toward each other from either side of the entrance. Through them, Sam observed the Stingray take off and hobble in the air. Moments later, they heard the shriek of the transport's abused engine fade as the craft moved away from Midgard and its surrounding fortifications.

"Who was that?" Dr. Gage asked in a strained voice.

"Jody Escobar, sir," Haskill replied. "She was the emergency pilot on the roster today."

The group of stunned bystanders winced at the concussion of a distant explosion. Stone-faced, Dr. Gage approached Haskill. "Was she able to eject?"

Haskill passed the question through his headset, and Sam tensed, waiting for the answer. "No word yet, sir. She was at least five kilometers out, though. I'll let you know once we find out."

"Okay. Thanks, Steve." Dr. Gage became aware that he had an attentive audience. "You and Sam come with me to the operations center. Steve, put all capsules on alert level one and ground all nonessential aircraft immediately until we find out how this happened. The rest of you will return to your stations. We still have a mission to do."

"Roger, sir." Haskill provided some instructions via his wristlet and noticed with irritation that some stragglers remained present. "You heard the boss, people. To your stations. Now." The remaining spectators dispersed into the corridor where silent red alarm lights blinked.

Sam followed Dr. Gage through the narrow hallways that connected the maze-like concentric corridors to the dome's center. *Not Jody, too,* he prayed silently.

Haskill shoved his way in front so he could override the identity authenticators that stood between them and the operations hub. The final door slid open and revealed a frenetic scene.

Several personnel clad in black and midnight blue huddled around an image of the Stingray as they argued about the nature and extent of the damage as well as the location of the impact points. Others looked at terrain models of the surprise tornado, and a few spoke to other security and intelligence analysts at the other capsules. Members of the defense force and the interior police had also piped in. The noise level increased as discussions about the incident became heated.

"I don't care about the damage report. I need to know what else was discovered at the storm's origination point."

"Hey, I can only do one thing at a time, Stan. What is the priority?"

"Transport damage analysis has priority."

"No, it doesn't! We need to find out more about that tornado!"

"Says who?

"Says the General. That's—" The intelligence analyst stopped mid-sentence as he caught sight of Dr. Gage, Steve Haskill, and Sam. The Director raised an eyebrow, and the room gradually went silent as people nudged and shushed each other.

Dr. Gage gave his audience a moment to collect themselves, but he was clearly displeased with the discord. He walked slowly to center stage and faced the assembled group. "All right, folks. We—all of us—have just experienced a significant traumatic event. We are all shocked and in pain and we cannot take that out on each other. Finding out what happened is not a competition. That kind of pettiness will get us nowhere. We need to focus on how we missed that storm, on who or what fired those missiles, and any other relevant threats to our sacred work. The only way we can answer those questions is if we withhold blame and shame and each of us does what we came here to do. Is that understood?"

"Yes, sir!" Everyone in the room and on the channels replied in unison. Sam observed looks of chagrin on several faces and defiance on others while others looked away, embarrassed.

"I am glad to hear it. I expect everyone to work together to find answers from this point forward, and that includes our government partners." He acknowledged the military and police contributors with a nod. "Pass along the word to everyone else." He turned to Haskill. "Steve, what can you tell us so far?"

Haskill stepped forward. "Sir, we were able to get a full schematic of the damage before we evacuated, and we have a team out looking for Escobar and the remnants of the transport right now."

Or the remnants of Jody Escobar. Sam felt an unwelcome surge of grief hit him like a punch to the solar plexus.

"Where, approximately, are they at the moment?"

Haskill nodded to one of the analysts, and she fiddled with her terminal. The optical netting dropped, and a diorama of Midgard, its defenses, and its restricted zone materialized. A cluster of blue figures appeared in the restricted zone.

"Very well," Dr. Gage said. "What did the transport's pilot report?"

"Not much yet, sir," Haskill replied. "He is in the clinic, but we will interview him as soon as he is stabilized."

"Fine. Get the big picture of what happened as soon as possible, but don't worry about the details until after he recovers. He did a heck of a job keeping the transport airborne given the circumstances."

Haskill grunted. "Well, sir, it appears he had some help. The Goshawk escorts we sent out said they were in radio contact with one of the passengers, who took over for the injured copilot. A guy named Hank or Chester or something like that."

"Was it Hector?" Sam interjected.

"It might have been. Why?" Haskill glared at Sam. He hated to be interrupted.

"He's a good friend of mine, and he was on that transport. And he knows how to fly just about everything in our fleet.

It is something he would do, too," Sam responded, surprised at the jealousy that came with that admission.

Dr. Gage gave Sam a strained smile. "It sounds like we may have a second hero for today along with Ms. Escobar. Good. We need a morale booster for everyone while we handle this travesty." The smile faded, and his jaw hardened. "After we get a sense for what—or who—is responsible."

He turned to the nearest analyst, a young brunette in the midnight blue of the intelligence cadre. "Hannah, what do we know so far?"

"Sir, our initial assessment is that this was a well-coordinated attack that involved precision weaponry fired from the ground, and it likely aimed to canalize the transport into this valley here." Hannah pointed to a graphical depiction of the area where the attack took place, which was peppered with red dots that templated the likely points of origin for the tornado as well as the missiles.

"And the tornado?" Gage asked, eyebrow raised.

Hannah flushed. "Sir, none of our weather analytics predicted cyclonic activity in that area. It was all supposed to be farther west."

Dr. Gage turned to Maria Amherst, the lead meteorologist. "Maria?"

She shook her head. "We're working on it, sir. Weather patterns have been shifting so radically lately that our algorithms have been unable to keep up. Although," she cautioned, "this instance is unusual."

Sam was only half-listening; he had figured out that much for himself already. Like a sleepwalker, he walked to the nearest open terminal and, over the next few minutes, pulled in area maps, historical weather information, and data on unrest, rebellion, terrorist, and guerrilla activity against Human Resiliency Program.

Meanwhile, Dr. Gage circled the attack schematic slowly as he took in details and asked further pointed questions. He turned to Haskill and said, “Steve, I want a full report on any wreckage or unusual imprints found at or near these sites.”

“Yes, sir, we’ll have all the details for you ahead of the crisis assembly this evening. So far, our recovery team has found some debris covered in a stealth coating we do not recognize. We’re analyzing samples of it now to determine who might have been involved. We have discovered that the munitions were not at all sophisticated. The fragments suggest it was a mild liquid explosive that would not have been powerful enough to penetrate the hull of an armored Stingray.”

Murmurs erupted throughout the room and on the screens as people digested this information and theorized about the weakness of the warheads.

Sam could have cared less about the weapons, but he ran a few models of the tornado on the terminal. His brow furrowed at the result, and he shook his head in denial and ran them again. However, the results pointed to the same disturbing conclusion. Dr. Gage located Sam and beckoned him forward.

“What do you think, Sam?” he asked. “Why didn’t the attackers use better warheads?”

The conversations stopped, and all heads turned toward Sam, who felt light-headed.

“Sir, whoever did this did not want to destroy the transport,” Sam responded. “They wanted to bring it down, and they used the tornado to move the Stingray into their trap.”

Dr. Gage and Haskill exchanged a significant look while others stared, trying to make sense of the words Sam had uttered.

"Sam, what do you mean 'they used the tornado to do it?'" Dr. Gage asked with eyes the hard blue of fluorite.

Sam inhaled and squared his shoulders. He had a premonition that what he had discovered might shatter any remaining sense of security. "Sir, whoever fired the missiles also created that tornado. Someone has the power to make their own weather."

CHAPTER SIXTEEN:

THE THREAT

Everyone—including the remote participants—stopped whatever they were doing and stared at Sam. Many appeared skeptical, and some sneered with disbelief. Sam was annoyed until he saw that Hannah, Don, and a handful of others who were familiar with his capabilities looked worried. Haskill's expression, however, registered lethal levels of irritation, and Sam recoiled when two members of the security team approached him. Fortunately, they stopped when Dr. Gage held up his hand.

"That won't be necessary, Steve."

The look of surprise on Haskill's face was so fleeting that Sam almost missed it before it was replaced by the security chief's habitual scowl. "Yes, sir!" he responded and signaled to the two guards, who resumed their positions at the door.

Dr. Gage put his hands behind his back and walked slowly toward Sam until he was directly in front of him.

"An interesting notion, Sam," he said in a deadly quiet voice, "but one that is highly improbable."

Sam opened his mouth to protest but clamped it shut when he saw the warning glint in the Director's eyes. *He knows. He knows and he wants to keep the information close hold for now.* Sam could not blame him. The enemy—whoever they were—had the ability to create storms on demand and combine them with a precision missile strike from a heavily fortified area. The implications for either were unnerving, but together they were downright terrifying.

He dropped his eyes to the floor. "True, sir. It is unlikely. My models are far from perfect due to—ah incomplete data and my lack of experience with these matters." The lie tasted bitter as it left his lips, especially when he saw disappointment on the faces of colleagues who, under normal circumstances, silently cheered him on.

"Yes, Sam, but that experience will come. I do appreciate your efforts, however." Dr. Gage met his eyes, and Sam saw an unspoken apology for the deception. The Director turned his face toward the audience around the room. In a raised voice, he continued, "And, on that note, we will leave you intelligence and weather experts to explore further theories as to how we missed both the tornado and the presence of missile launch sites so near our headquarters."

A chorus of, "Yes, sir," echoed off the walls and in the ceiling. "Good. We will reconvene in two hours, and I want some answers. Steve, Don, Sam—with me, please."

The guards stepped aside to let the Director through, and the room slowly came back to life after his exit. Uncomfortable mutters and murmurs followed Sam as he trailed his mentor.

The main corridor thronged with clumps of people. Some of them held whispered conferences, and many looked scared. They moved aside and went silent as the Director approached. With gravity, he acknowledged their respectful silence, and his demeanor and quick words of encouragement reassured most of them that everything was under control.

Even if it isn't.

Resentment simmered inside Sam as he trailed in Dr. Gage's wake. He knew he was right—or was close to the truth—and, while the deceit might prevent unnecessary anxiety in the short term, the danger his theory presented to the entire Capsule enterprise could not be hidden for very long.

Rayna waited for them in the leadership suite and ushered them into Dr. Gage's office. "The Capsule directors and security chiefs will be up and ready for you in one hour, sir."

"Thanks, Rayna," Dr. Gage said. "This discussion won't take long. I need to go over some new communications protocols with you when I'm finished as a precaution."

"Yes, sir, I'll be waiting." Her voice shook. *She's rattled, too,* Sam thought. *And she knows he's shaken.*

They followed the Director into his office, and in response to his instructions, Don went to the terminal while Sam and Steve Haskill joined him at the table. Dr. Gage responded to a message on his wristlet but looked up to observe Sam, who thrummed with anticipation as he looked nervously back and forth between his mentor and the security chief. Both had a menacing demeanor that made Sam want to disappear.

"The General is not available on a secure channel right now, sir," Don called over his shoulder. "He's out with a strike team."

"Fine. I'll touch base with him later." He leaned forward and rested his chin in his hands in a posture that Sam recognized immediately. It was the position he used when he had to impart something unpleasant to a subordinate.

"All right, Sam. Tell me everything you know about storm generators."

"Ahem." Sam's mouth suddenly felt dry. "Not much, sir. We, uh, we learned about them at the academy in our environmental history course. Ostensibly, their purpose was to counter dangerous weather patterns. They were modeled on the same concept as back-burning wildfires, and I think the idea was that, when used against a high-category tornado or hurricane, a smaller, more controlled storm could cause the large one to dissipate or, at a minimum, lessen its severity. But… well, they uh—"

"Go on, Sam," Dr. Gage encouraged, but his eyes bored into Sam's like drills.

Sam licked his lips. "But some countries manipulated the technology to change weather patterns in their favor. They would move rain clouds and such from one country to another and things like that. And—" He waited for Dr. Gage to stop him. When he did not, Sam continued, "And they were outlawed decades ago during the International Climate Convention after some countries tried to weaponize storms for use against their adversaries."

To Sam's surprise, the Director was not upset. "Yes, Sam, that's right. The United States was guilty of abusing that technology. Though, that bit of history was… adjusted for public consumption. But," he raised a finger, "that was before we signed the Weather Exploitation Treaty." He sighed and sat back in his chair. "My father personally supervised the destruction of our stockpile and all—and I do mean all—of the associated design information."

Sam strongly suspected that if Dr. Gage's father was anything like his other son, the folks with the technical expertise had also been destroyed, and he cringed.

"The thing is, Sam, even the most advanced storm generation technology of the time was incapable of generating a precision tornado, least of all one immune to meteorological surveillance."

"Yes, sir, but it's the only explanation for a spontaneous, precision tornado like that."

"Are you sure, Sam?"

Sam did not hesitate. "Absolutely. If you would like to see my models, sir, Don can pull them from the folder I set up in my personal archives."

Without waiting for directions, Don fingered the terminal's interface. His eyes widened at what he saw before he diverted the results to the optical netting, which lowered from the ceiling. "Unbelievable," he whispered under his breath, mesmerized by the screen.

"Yes, it is," Dr. Gage responded, fascinated by the simulation. The three-dimensional image of Midgard's cupola glittered to his right. Rounded, barren peaks of the Blue Ridge mountains were to its east, illuminated by a blue line that showed the Stingray's planned flight path into the capsule. As the Stingray and its Goshawk escorts entered Midgard's restricted zone, an inverted cone of swirling winds rose up from the ground. In less than a minute, the sky around the transport turned black, and the vortex swallowed an escort. At that precise point, the craft veered right into a valley, and the first of two projectiles launched from the valley floor. The craft staggered and straightened before the second volley hit, again on the starboard side. The Stingray looked doomed but, at the last minute, the pilot—*or Hector*—pulled it out of a dive and steered it back toward the dome.

"Show it again," the Director commanded. The group watched the virtual demonstration three more times, and Dr. Gage's face looked more like his brother's stony visage with each successive viewing.

"Do you have any theories as to who perpetrated the attack?"

"I've started working on that as well, sir, though I have not completed my analysis." Sam stood up and exchanged places with Don at the terminal. The digital attack model disappeared. In its place was a three-dimensional view of North America with a multitude of red, orange, and yellow of varying size scattered across it like atomic particles.

Sam fingered the screen, and all save some red dots in Canada and a handful in the United States disappeared. "As we've discussed, our neighbors to the north have an interest in our program, but they have not—at least to my knowledge—extended that competition to acts of violence. The cursory search I was able to do from our limited intelligence archives showed no indication that they have a storm generator. That said, they do have the resources to build one, and, if it is true that they are trying to take over our northern capsules, they have the motivation to do so. Moreover, their special forces are capable of conducting complex operations like the one demonstrated here, but we would have known if they crossed the border." He met Dr. Gage's astonished face. "If it is Canada, they likely used a domestic armed group as a proxy to conduct the attack."

Sam touched the screen again and clusters of orange dots flared across the United States near more populous cities and locales. "Several US-based actors are capable of conducting the ground attack. They include—"

But Haskill had jumped to his feet and almost choked on his own venom. "Anyone in there would have had to break past our defenses in that area, and—"

The Director raised his eyebrows, which silenced him. "Yes, Steve, it is a restricted area, one that has likely been breached and probably by an insider. I'll leave that one to you to investigate unless—" He turned his attention back toward Sam.

But Sam shook his head. "Sir, I don't have access to the security rotation information. I agree that the attackers had inside assistance, but as you say, Mr. Haskill is the best choice to run that one down."

"Or my brother," Dr. Gage said dryly.

This comment seemed to infuriate rather than mollify Haskill, but he returned to his seat.

"Continue please, Sam."

"Yes, sir. The Domestic groups who have the organization, skills, and access to weapons to conduct the ground attack include terrorist and guerilla organizations like the Watichis and Natronas.However, their typical modus operandi does not involve targeting passengers or people. They tend to go after weapons, rations, and medical supplies, but they like to enflame dissonant activity as a distraction while they do so."

Small specks of blue glowed brightly on the simulation. "And as I am sure Mr. Haskill is aware, there is an insider threat from other Human Resiliency Projects. The Mars Project in particular faced cutbacks after their second shuttle exploded last year, and they have people with access to the Capsule program records."

The corner of Dr. Gage's mouth went down. "They wouldn't dare," he said.

"I wouldn't know, sir," Sam responded, but his attitude suggested the idea was worth looking into. He tapped the screen again and the purple smudges on the map became prominent. "Other culprits could involve some of the un-Tiered local defense like the Chicago Indigent Force or the Minneapolis dissidents, or—"

Dr. Gage shook his head vigorously. "No way could that rabble be capable of designing a storm generator, let alone building one."

Sam paused to consider his next words. "I am not so sure about that, sir. We know very little about those people since the government only cares if and when they become disruptive or violent. There are many innovative, creative types in that crowd, including former graphic designers, architects, sculptors, writers, and even scientists and technologists who might have been downgraded for poor health or performance. My recommendation is to look more closely at the people in these areas…" he waved to the orange glows across the continent, "to identify and locate prospective leaders or contacts with the local armed groups and, perhaps, international actors as well."

"Perhaps," the Director responded, though his voice was heavy with doubt. "But why would anyone in those groups want to destroy one of our transports? To send a message perhaps? Wanton destruction doesn't seem to fit here."

"Sir, remember, that whoever they are wanted to get the Stingray on the ground, not destroy it." He tapped the screen again and an image of the Stingray appeared templated with the location of the two projectile hits. Sam left the terminal and went to the display. "See this first hit here? A more powerful explosive would have penetrated the hull. This hit did not, and neither did the next one. Moreover, the missiles were fired from the valley floor, indicating the presence of people there—who wanted to take someone—or something—onboard."

"They would not have needed to penetrate the hull to cause a crash landing," the Director remarked.

"True, sir, but I think that second hit was mistimed." Sam pulled back up the original terrain model with the Stingray on its original flight path. He paused the simulation after the first hit and pointed to the ground. "The second hit came from here—" he pointed, and the second projectile fired, "but the ground there is not level with a significant elevation change between those two locations. I suspect they rehearsed their attack on more level ground, or they planned the attack for a different location and changed their mind."

Sam went to the terminal and adjusted the simulation. This time, the Stingray made it closer to Midgard before the first hit to the starboard side, and the second missile hit the port side of the aircraft. "That projectile caused the transport to spiral before someone on board was able to level it out."

At Sam's touch, figurines in all-terrain ground vehicles jumped out, invaded the aircraft, and exfiltrated with an unknown person or persons. "The only piece of the analysis I have not completed," Sam continued, "is why they chose the valley instead of the flats. They'd have had less concealment there, but their operation would have been more successful."

Dr. Gage and Haskill looked at each other. Both were surprised, and Sam could have sworn he saw fear momentarily cross the Director's face. Don, too, was frozen, and he looked at Sam as if he had suddenly sprung wires out of his ears.

"Sam, there's no need to continue along that line of thought. I don't want to risk anyone else duplicating your assessment." In response to Sam's astonished look, he continued, "I'll tell you what is there soon enough. It's a carefully guarded secret and, if what you say is true, that secret might have been compromised."

Silence fell, but it was the loudest silence Sam could remember.

Dr. Gage watched the updated simulation twice more. "Who do you think they wanted on that transport, Sam?"

"Tamara Ashraf, sir. She's got this—"

"Natural genetic resiliency. Yes, I know. That is part of the reason I agreed to bring her into Capsule despite her lackluster test results."

I'll bet my mother let him know, Sam thought ruefully but forced his face to remain even keeled.

"I wonder—" Dr. Gage mused aloud. Then he shook his head. "Gentlemen, this is a game changer. Right now, Steve, I want to know who had access to the flight manifest, the flight path information, and who might be aware of our secret activities in the restricted zone."

So, I am right, Sam thought.

"What additional defense mechanisms have we put in place, Steve?"

"Our forces are on the highest alert, and we now have some assistance from the interior police and the military. They know the stakes, and they are prepared to support us in the event of an—incursion."

Silence ensued. Everyone present knew how little help those defenses would be against an enemy who could harness the power of Mother Nature.

Haskill decided to channel his discomfort into malice, "Of course, if Richmond here is right, we need to prepare to defend against an army of indigents."

"Drop it, Steve," Dr. Gage ordered.

"Yes, sir," Haskill said, but Sam knew from the look on Haskill's face that he had made an implacable enemy.

"In the meantime, have your teams continue their search for signs of other humans in Midgard's restricted zone. Feel free to consult with the General and his forces as well. You have my permission to go direct with him for the time being. You can leave us now."

"Yes, sir." Haskill stood rigidly to attention and left while Sam maintained his seat and tried to shake off the feeling of dread.

"You continue to amaze me, Sam," Dr. Gage said. "But you need to be careful."

"Yes, sir, I can see that now." He knew from his past engagements with the General and, more recently Steve Haskill, that he was perilously close to an "accident."

Dr. Gage pressed his hands over his face in agitation. "Frankly, I am tired of keeping things from you, Sam. The truth is that I feel protective of you, and sometimes I forget you are very much your own person and not just your mother's son. After today's events, it is clear to me that it is both foolish and futile to shield you from anything else. My apologies for doing you—and our mission—a disservice."

Sam felt queasy. Dr. Gage was apologizing to *him?* "No apology is necessary, sir."

"I sincerely wish that were true, Sam. I've endangered everyone who works for me, including your friends. What I can promise you is that, if you help me, you will have the opportunity for retribution."

They sat in an uncomfortable silence. Abruptly, Gage leaned forward. "I know it is late, but you should go check on your friends now. I've given you authorization to enter the clinic. Just stay out of the way of the medical professionals. Then get a few hours of sleep. I need you in my office at zero four hundred tomorrow."

“Yes, sir,” Sam responded. He hesitated. “Should I pack?”

Dr. Gage smiled wryly. “No, Sam, Don here can take care of your belongings. I need you completely focused and ready for your indoctrination.”

CHAPTER SEVENTEEN:

THE PROPOSAL

Midgard's medical clinic was located in its own pod outside of the main dome. Its inconvenient placement was due to the need to isolate any contagious patients or rogue pathogens from the main enterprise. Each capsule had duplicate medical staffs who were prohibited from working together for the same reason, even in emergencies like this one.

Sam noted the abnormally high patient-to-caregiver ratio as he stepped from the decontamination chamber into the cramped treatment area.

The room pulsed with unpleasant sights and sounds. People screamed and moaned. Medical staff shouted orders over the din. Doctors and nurses waded from the medical supply cabinets to their patients and back again. Physiological monitoring devices sounded alarms in asynchronous increments until a frazzled technician yelled, "Turn those damn things off!" However, the sudden cessation of alarms only served to amplify the other noises of the triage scene.

Once Sam adjusted to the volume level, his other senses took over. The smell—*Oh, God, the smell.* The sweet, putrid scent of burnt flesh on top of blood, sweat, and other bodily odors permeated the space. Sam tasted bile in his mouth and staggered. A team of two medical staff with a bulky burn treatment device moved past, and he hastily grabbed a discarded sample tray. He used it to capture the contents of his stomach as it heaved again and again, adding the rankness of his vomit to the rest of the fetid bouquet.

"Hey there, buddy." Someone with a soot-streaked hand in a strange pattern held a towel in front of his face. *I've seen that mark somewhere before,* Sam thought irreverently as he accepted the towel, wiped his mouth, and placed the tray on a nearby table.

Hector stood before him with a wry smile on his blackened face. Dirt, blood, and debris matted his golden-brown curls, and lines of exhaustion and worry framed his aqua eyes. The smile, though genuine, was a façade for the trauma he had just experienced.

"Thanks, Hector," Sam said weakly. "Anyone would think I am supposed to be the patient instead of you. I'm so sorry—"

"Don't worry about it, bud. I've felt worse. Head wounds always bleed a lot. I've been waiting for you so I could take you to see Tam. She's been asking about you since she woke up. But, when I saw you turn that fabulous shade of green, I knew I had to move fast." He grinned and clapped Sam on the shoulder.

"She's stable then," Sam exhaled and felt his knees go weak with relief. "Why don't you take me over and then get yourself looked at?"

"That's my plan." Hector's eyes tightened as he swept the room. "This is pretty bad, huh?"

"The worst I've seen," Sam agreed. "The generator accident at Durango last fall was bad, but it was nothing like this." He did not add that he had seen plenty of disfigurations and disease-related mutilations in his mother's clinic growing up, along with several injuries and deaths at Midgard from accidents, natural disasters, and grisly suicide attempts. But he had never witnessed a mass casualty event of this scale.

"I wish I could say the same. But it wouldn't be true." Hector looked sadly at the carnage.

Sam had never seen Hector so distressed, and he felt an unfamiliar urge to comfort him. "This isn't your fault, you know," he said carefully. "If it hadn't been for you, no one would have survived. You're a hero."

"Don't be so sure about that," Hector retorted. He put one hand over his face. "I'm sorry, Sam. I know you're trying to help, but I don't want to talk about it." He shuddered convulsively, collected himself, and pointed to the far corner of the pod. "Tam is right over there—near the window. Follow me."

He slipped through the chaos with balanced ease while Sam did his best to follow without knocking over medical equipment, doctors, or patients. When they arrived at Tamara's bed, he saw that she was encased in a cylindrical contraption from the chest down. The remnants of her dark curls lay tangled on the pillow, and ashy, tear-streaked smudges framed her enormous brown eyes. He looked closer and saw that her pupils were enlarged and her gaze unfocused.

"Yes, she has been drugged. You guys at Midgard have the best narcotics the government can supply." The joke failed to hide Hector's anxiety.

"Hey, Tam," Sam said gently. "I heard you guys had one heck of a ride. How do you feel?"

She grinned and rolled her eyes. "Amazing. No, seriously, I feel like I'm floating right now. It kinda reminds me of zero gravity training. What the hell did your people do to me, Samuel?"

Sam cringed at her use of the expletive and his full first name, which she typically saved for times of extreme ire, but he kept his tone light. "Trust me, you don't want to know what they gave, and the pain eliminators are a closely guarded secret anyhow."

"Speaking of pain," Hector interjected, "she has two broken ribs, a dislocated shoulder, and some intense burns on her back and arm. If she behaves herself, she will be up and moving in a week or two, but she'll probably need to stay here for a while. Or that's what the good doctor over there told me." He jerked his head in the direction of an attractive, older woman in the cobalt blue uniform of the medical staff,

Hector leaned into Sam and murmured, "Do you think you can work your magic and give her the chance to recoup here? The rehabilitation facilities at Midgard are much better than at Phoenix."

"You know," Tamara said loudly, "it is pretty damn rude to talk about me like I'm not just lying here. And while we're on the topic, Sam, I would feel so much better if you can get Mr. Tough Guy to get his wounds taken care of instead of talking trash about me."

Sam grinned. "I can manage both requests easily. Dr. Malika," he called to the female doctor, who looked at Hector as if she wanted to pounce, "I'd like to introduce you to my friend, Hector Ramirez. As you can see, he needs medical attention and probably a mental evaluation too." He deadpanned the last line so well that the doctor might have acted on both issues had Hector not gently punched him in the shoulder and laughed.

"Don't listen to this guy. He has it in for me."

Dr. Malika apprised Hector's impressive—if somewhat battered—figure and gave him a coquettish side-eye. "Thanks, Mr. Richmond. I've been waiting to treat your friend here since he arrived in my clinic, but he refused to leave this young woman's side until now."

Hector returned her flirty attitude with the appearance of bashfulness, but Sam knew better. So did Tamara. She rolled her eyes and shook her head as Hector said, "Well, now that you have someone else to make sure you take your medicine, I guess I will go with the nice doctor." He gently smoothed Tamara's hair back from her head in an intimate gesture that took Sam by surprise before he attributed it to their recent near-death experience. "I'll catch up with you later, pal, though I'm sure you've heard the whole story by now."

Before Sam could respond, Hector turned and gave Dr. Malika a bright, false smile. "Anyhow, it is past time for me to get this ugly little cut taken care of. I'll see you both later."

Sam stared after him. *Why is he so upset?* Certainly, the attack was harrowing for all of them, but Hector did not seem at all pleased with the fact that he had salvaged several lives by his actions.

A movement from Tamara broke his contemplation, and he turned toward her. "Dr. Malika seems to have taken a shine to Hector already."

Instead of sharing his conspiratorial smile, Tamara grimaced, and her eyes welled with tears.

"What's wrong?" he asked. "Are you in pain? Hang on, I'll get someone to help—"

"No, Sam, please don't. It's just that, um..." She paused and looked down, and Sam got the impression she was about to deliver some unpleasant news. "I feel so helpless lying here."

She's dodging me, Sam realized. *Whatever she wants to tell me must be pretty bad.* "Tam, what is it? You can tell me anything. You know that."

She avoided his eyes, and he decided to switch tactics until he could maneuver the conversation back to the source of her distress.

"Very well, we can discuss whatever is bothering you later. I have a surprise for you, one I hope you will like. If nothing else, it will give you something positive to think about while you recover."

Tamara's relief was palpable. "A surprise? For me?"

"Did you ever meet Audrey Shin? She works here at Midgard, but she's been to Phoenix a few times."

Confused, Tamara responded, "Yes, I think so. She's a harvester, right? We've collaborated with her team recently."

Sam nodded. "Yes, you have. Anyhow, Audrey just accepted a promotion, and she's moving to the Nashua capsule in five months. Dr. Gage wants to fill her vacancy with an experienced harvester instead of waiting for a newbie from the next Accessions cycle."

He waited for Tamara to catch the implication, and he was not disappointed. Her eyes widened. "Ohhhhh."

The words gushed out of Sam's mouth like a geyser. "I spoke with Dr. Gage about you, and he wants to sign off on a special move to bring you here to Midgard. Permanently. I know you've had a rough spell in Phoenix, but we have better materials and facilities for you to work with here, and there is more leeway for experimentation and new techniques. You—you could sort of start fresh here if—if you wanted to."

But Tamara's expression indicated that all she wanted to do was crawl right out of her container.

Why isn't she more excited? Sam was puzzled. Automatically, his hand reached into his pocket and brought out the oval-shaped metal container that he had stowed there prior to his flying lesson that morning—ages ago by the measure of events since then. He removed a silvery chain with his mother's pendant from inside, and Tamara's eyes grew wider still. Jewelry was impossible to acquire unless one had family connections... or heirlooms.

"It belonged to my mother," Sam explained. "She gave it to me the day she disappeared." A warm glow started in Sam's solar plexus and spread outward, and he felt like she was there with him, giving him her approval. "She told me I would know who to give it to. I knew it was meant for you when we were at Lake Tahoe together, but I didn't have it with me then." He held the bauble toward Tamara. "You don't need to decide anything now, but that harvester position is a great opportunity for you and," he took a deep breath to steady his voice, "...and we could be together. I mean, well, if you wanted to. I mean I'd like us to be together. When I was with you in January, I realized that—"

"Sam, stop it. Please just stop." Tamara shook her head, winced, and stilled. "Put it back, please. It's lovely, and I know what you're asking me, but I can't."

His veins, which had flooded with warmth, now turned to ice. "Can't? Or won't?"

Her jaw tightened as she strove to hold back the flood. "Sam, I didn't want you to find out this way, believe me. I was going to tell you this week while I was here." She closed her eyes, inhaled, and blurted, "Hector and I are dating. We've been together for months."

Her words were so unexpected that, for a moment, Sam could not process them. "What!"

Tamara's chin wobbled. "I'm so, so sorry, Sam. I didn't want to hurt you but—" She tried to shrug but cringed and stopped.

Sam attempted to clear his head. "So," he said slowly. "You're in love with Hector." When she did not respond, he repeated, "With Hector."

"Yes, Sam," she said quietly, "I am."

The world shifted under Sam's feet, and he swayed. Fortunately, a chair was nearby, so he sat himself firmly on it while he attempted to recover from the blow to his soul. They sat together in silence for what felt like hours while he strategized, and she wished herself millions of miles away from the pain she saw on his features.

"Look," he started slowly, calmly, "I know I may have missed my shot here, but the thing is, Tam, I know now that I love you for you and not because of your ties to my past. I want to be with you, and I have this vision of us together, working and living here, and maybe even applying for a reproductive license or—"

"Sam, please don't," Tam pleaded as she remembered her bizarre daydream from just before the attack.

"No, wait. Just let me finish before you make any decisions. I know you cared about me for ages, and I kept you at arm's length, but I am confident you loved me." He paused to swallow. "Perhaps you still do. I just felt like I had nothing to offer you—you know—emotionally, until this past January." He grabbed his hair in agitation. "Is there even a small chance you might want to be with me now that you know how I feel? Because, if there is, I will wait and give you and Hector space to figure things out. I'll wait until Capsule goes into full launch mode if I have to. I just need to know that it is possible you'll change your mind."

Tamara gave up and let the tears fall. "Sam, did you ever wonder why I never told you how I felt?" Her voice was choked.

Misery settled on Sam like fog into a valley. "Because I never gave you the chance."

"Yes," she nodded, "that is part of it. You hold things so close, Sam, that it is hard for anyone to get in, even when they're beating down on the door to the fortress you've erected around your feelings. So, I waited for some sign that you wanted something more than friendship from me, and I thought I saw a spark at Tahoe. But then you got distracted and—"

"'Yes," said Sam dully. "I remember."

"Anyways, when we were waiting in the Falconet to return to Phoenix, I watched the two of you interact in the cockpit," she admitted. "I don't remember exactly what you were talking about, but you looked serious, like you always do, and he tried to tease you into relaxing. It was strange, but I felt my feelings for you begin to shift to him."

Sam bit his upper lip and nodded. He vaguely remembered the conversation but had missed its underlying significance.

Tamara looked down at her containerized body. "We applied for a formal authorization to be a couple last month, Sam. The Phoenix director just informed us that the approval is in the works. Hector's promotion helped speed the process." She bit her lip. "We plan to marry early next year."

Funny, thought Sam, *she makes it sound so clinical, as if they submitted a request for supplies or something.* The fiery, passionate Tam had decided to join with someone whose zest for life—and love—far exceeded his own but spoke about it in terms better suited to a checklist than a romance.

Even so, it felt as final as it sounded, and Sam condemned himself for being too absorbed in his work and general ennui to take the one chance he had at happiness. Anguish would come later, he knew. But, for now, he was numbed by all of the shocks the day had brought.

"Very well, Tam," he said flatly. "You've made your choice. I hope you and Hector will be happy together."

To Tamara, it sounded more like Sam wished they would both just jump off the nearest precipice. "Please try to understand, Sam. It's the best thing for all three of us."

"You certainly seem to think so." The crushed look on her already strained face made him momentarily regret his harshness, but he wanted—needed—to stay in control for himself as much as for the curious onlookers around the clinic. He waved over one of the medical attendants.

"You need to rest," he said to Tamara. "I will ensure that you get everything you need and that you can complete your recovery here so you can return to full health. If Hector the Hero wants to remain with you while you convalesce, I will arrange for him to do so." He held up his hand to stop her protest. "I won't interfere, but I need time and space to adjust to the new... circumstances of our relationship." Sam was pleased with the cool professionalism with which he spoke, except for the jibe against Hector.

"Oh, Sam," Tamara breathed softly as the attendant injected more sedatives into her bloodstream. "I will miss you." Her eyes oozed tears as they fluttered and then closed.

Without any indication that he had heard her, Sam brusquely moved into the airlock with the pendant clutched tightly in his fisted hand.

CHAPTER EIGHTEEN:

THE INDOCTRINATION

It was daytime, and Sam was in the restricted zone near where the transport was attacked. He was part of the survey team looking for evidence of a storm generator. Although they were surrounded by mountains, rock formations, and thick "ghost forests" of dead trees, the sun burned down so brightly that it pained him. He looked down at his hands and saw, with dismay, they had blistered in the intense heat. The sores on his left hand were in the form of a shape that he recognized but was unable to place. *It's at the wrong angle*, he thought. *Bizarre.*

Before he could ponder that unbidden thought further, he realized with a start that, unlike the rest of the team, he was not in his protective suit. He turned back toward the valley to gauge the distance to the nearest checkpoint and cursed when he realized it was at least a mile away. *I won't make it before I succumb to heat exhaustion,* he thought.

However, when he looked around to ask for help, he found that he was alone. He checked the tracking mechanism on his wristlet, but no blue figures were anywhere in his vicinity. Sam's anxiety level increased as he ascended a steep slope toward the checkpoint. The exposed skin on his face and hands seared with pain, and the perspiration that trickled down his face stung the open wounds.

Was it his imagination or had the checkpoint moved farther away? It looked smaller. *I'm hallucinating. Maybe I should find shelter and wait until someone comes.*

"Sam! Sam! Over here!"

Energized by hope, Sam followed the sound of Tamara's voice. She was behind him on the valley floor in a protective suit, her helmet, strangely, was in her hands. But she otherwise looked well. Too well, in fact. *How did she heal so quickly?*

"Come on, Sam! I've called a transport to pick us up. You have to hurry or you'll miss it!"

The urgency in her voice propelled Sam to action, and he stumbled through brush and ash toward her. The shadow of a Stingray hovered overhead, and the craft settled down behind Tamara. When its hatch lowered to the ground, a familiar figure loped down the ramp.

"Jody?" he yelled, hoarsely. "Jody! You're alive!"

"Of course I am, Richmond. Did you think a little explosion would keep me down? I came to save your tail as usual." She smiled at him and winked.

"Hurry up, Sam! We have to go now." Tamara's voice was insistent. She joined Jody on the dropped hatch and stepped backward up the ramp.

"I'm almost there," Sam panted, but they, too, now seemed to be moving away from him. "Wait for me. Please!" he cried.

Tamara looked sorrowful. "It's too late, Sam. We have to go before the storm comes." She and Jody turned toward each other and then, together, marched up the ramp.

"When is it coming?" Sam asked, but no one heard him. The hatch folded into the bottom of the transport, and the Stingray lifted and then sped off toward Midgard. Sam dropped to his knees and put his hands out in supplication. The wind picked up and the sunlight dimmed as the sky turned a dark blackish green. A venomous-looking whirlwind rose up from the ground and, before Sam's eyes, first chased and then consumed the silvery disc.

"No!" Sam screamed. "No!"

A raw, harsh sensation in the back of his throat woke Sam from his nightmare. Sheets dampened by his cold sweat constricted him, and he had to wrest himself from them while he called for light. With the illumination came relief. *It was just a dream.*

The respite was short-lived, however, as the memories of the previous day's events thrust him back into a desolate reality. Sam mentally tallied them against the backdrop of his terrible dream. There was the appalling Stingray attack, Jody's last sacrificial act, Stephan Gage's frustration and confusion, and Tamara's rejection—all of which occurred within hours of one another. And underlying all of them was a new revelation that put further cracks in the foundations of Sam's world.

Dr. Gage had to have known that Tamara and Hector planned to marry, as he was the approval authority for all of Capsule's permanent partnerships. *He let me plan for the future, knowing those plans would never come to fruition.* In some respects, it was a far worse betrayal than Tamara's defection. A sick misery settled on his spirit, and he almost wished himself back in the dream rather than his new reality—a lifetime spent in enclosed environments, barricaded against threats from weather and rabble without Tamara, Jody, or anyone else for companionship. He would find no refuge from the coming tedium apart from the occasional crisis.

He exhaled and checked the time. 0332. He had just under half an hour before his scheduled indoctrination, and his hands went clammy when he hypothesized about what it would entail. Physical pain? Another series of emotional tests? A brain-penetrating scan? None of them were pleasant but, he reminded himself, they were unlikely to be worse than what he had experienced in the past eighteen hours.

What is that expression? It was something about the world seeming darker in the hours before dawn. Whatever it was fit his mood precisely. He hoped that this new mission would lead him down a brighter path where he would find some other reason—or person—to keep him going.

He sifted through his meager belongings to identify and set aside the items that would follow him to wherever he would move to after his indoctrination. In one of the desk's drawers, he found the folder in which he had saved Miranda's handwritten note from that terrible day when she had left. But it was caught in the space between the desktop, and he had to yank it out. The oval box containing the pendant flew off the desk, and Sam scrambled to retrieve it.

You will know who to give it to. Miranda's words echoed through his mind as he retrieved the box and examined its contents. Here was a tangible example of his failure to understand her at all. He had not, as it turned out, offered it to the right person after all. But he still admired the imprint of nature's perfect spiral as it glittered in the palm of his hand.

A jolt of recognition rushed through him with electric energy. *I just saw this symbol somewhere else.* He closed his eyes and let images float through his thoughts as if they were laid out on a digital diorama. Miranda's sad, pensive face when she gave it to him came to mind and, close on its heels, was Tamara's look of longing when she rejected the object—and his proposal. Tamara's eyes in his dream had looked just as melancholy as when she had left him alone in the wilderness. She had ignored his wild waving hands and—

Hands. That's where the symbol was.

Shocked, Sam examined his left hand. He saw no trace of the blistering from his dream nor any scarring or other skin irregularities. Yet Sam was certain he had seen that same pattern on his own hand in the dream.

The reminder on his wristlet beeped, and Sam swore and hastened the process of organizing his things. He took one last look around his room before he left it—possibly for good. It could have belonged to anyone. Apart from the satchel containing his belongings, he saw no indication he had been there. He vowed that his life would not share its fate before he closed and sealed the door.

Midgard's corridors had a strange feel about them. Sam saw people huddled near doorways making urgent conversations in low voices, though those ceased when they saw him approach. He sighed to himself, tired of the fact that, for most of Midgard's personnel, his presence signified an interruption rather than a welcome. A change of scene was clearly overdue.

The hall displays outside of Dr. Gage's office caught his attention. They flashed images of those who had perished, Jody's among them. Her picture showed her seated in a Goshawk Interceptor, and under it was her name and details of her death. *Escobar, Judith: Killed in Stingray explosion.* Sam was appalled. This memorial was devoid of Jody's vibrant, lively personality. He tightened his chin. *She deserved better.*

Still melancholy, Sam entered his office and almost jumped out of his skin when he saw Don sitting at his desk.

"Whoa there, Sam. Sorry I scared you. The boss asked me to take over my old job today since you're headed out. Is your stuff packed?"

"Yes," Sam responded, though his heart still hammered. "It's on my bunk."

"Perfect. I'll see that it joins you at your new assignment."

"Thank you," Sam responded, knowing that any further inquiries would have to wait. "Is the Director ready for me?"

"Yes, but before you go in, I want to run something by you. You said Hector Ramirez is a friend of yours. Right?"

The green-eyed monster reared up inside Sam, and he fought to keep it down. "Yes," he said through gritted teeth. "He is." *Or, rather, was.*

Oblivious to Sam's stilted voice, Don continued with enthusiasm. "What do you think about having him fill in for you while you're away? I found someone able to stand in for him as Phoenix's physical endurance director. Dr. Gage mentioned Hector's name when we looked at viable replacements for you, and his record is stellar."

Sam felt physically sick. Hector was basically the new and improved Sam as far as Tamara, Dr. Gage, and everyone else was concerned. He scrutinized Don, but he appeared unaware of the love triangle he had stumbled upon.

"Yes," he responded harshly, "Hector is a great guy, and he would be a superb fit for the role." Don looked taken aback by the severity of the response, and Sam strove to control his emotion. "That reminds me. Hector and I have a mutual friend, Tamara Ashraf, who was injured during yesterday's attack. It—uh—would be better for her to stay here and recover, especially if a friendly face is around. Can you see about keeping her here?"

"Of course," Don said, relieved when he thought he understood the source of Sam's vexation. "I'd forgotten. Ms. Ashraf is your ah—"

"Friend," Sam said emphatically. "But nothing more."

Don was sympathetic but knew better than to embarrass Sam further by showing it. "Got it. I will ask Dr. Gage, but I don't think it will be a problem." He jerked his head toward the Director's office "You can go in now. He's waiting for you."

When Sam stepped over the threshold, he observed Dr. Gage reviewing some material on his tablet. He looked up when Sam entered and motioned for him to take a seat while he tapped in some notes. "I'll be with you in a moment, Sam. Steve Haskill is on his way."

"Yes, sir."

Despite his efforts to mask his feelings, the resentment underlying those two simple words was unmistakable. Dr. Gage gave Sam a stern glance over the top of his tablet before returning his attention to its contents. After a moment, he said, "You need to get past your personal feelings, Sam, and you need to do so in short order. Frankly, you should have seen Ms. Ashraf's decision coming."

"Yes, perhaps I should have," Sam said, tight-lipped.

Dr. Gage sighed, shook his head, and set the tablet down. He raised his head and met Sam's hostile eyes, his gaze softening. "I looked in on Ms. Ashraf and Mr. Ramirez at the clinic this morning. They are both doing well, though she'll have to spend at least a week in the skin grafter. Dr. Malika informed me that she expects a full recovery for them both."

Sam broke eye contact because he could not trust himself to speak. Dr. Gage continued, "I did not think it was my place to tell you about Ms. Ashraf's application, Sam. Believe me, I took no joy anticipating your heartbreak."

The pity and concern in his voice were unwelcome, but it helped to mitigate some of Sam's angst. "I know, sir. It is just hard to accept that on top of everything else—" He broke off, unable to continue.

"Unfortunately, my boy, your path will only get harder from here. But I can tell you that your ability to handle physical and emotional trauma will improve as you experience more of both."

The moment broke when Steve Haskill entered carrying a small cylindrical device and a biometric scanner. "Is he ready, sir?"

"Yes, I am," Sam responded as he stood up. *Clearly Haskill is still pissed that I upstaged him yesterday.* But Sam had neither the time nor inclination to smooth that relationship now.

Haskill grunted and joined Gage at the table. Sam took the seat to Gage's left perhaps, he thought, for the last time in months. Or ever.

"Okay, Sam," Dr. Gage began. "You are about to be exposed to some very sensitive information. Less than forty people in the entire Capsule program are privy to this material, apart from my brother and his security force, of course." He leaned toward Sam. "There is no backing out of this program once you are indoctrinated. Unauthorized disclosure of any of this information will mean life imprisonment at a minimum for you and anyone you leak the information to, inadvertently or otherwise. Do you understand?"

Sam felt dizzy. "Life imprisonment at a minimum" was frequently a pseudonym for "immediate termination." But there was no going back now, not after yesterday. "I understand," he whispered.

"Do you agree to these conditions?" Dr. Gage was insistent.

There was only one answer. "Yes, sir, I agree to the conditions."

"Good," Dr. Gage said and clasped his hands together. *He seems relieved,* Sam thought, confused.

"Steve, if you would please do the honors." He gestured to Haskill, who plopped the scanner down on the table in front of Sam.

"Place your right hand here and hold it steady, Richmond," he sneered. Sam complied, and the scanner burned blue and warmed as it connected with his palm. The device hummed pleasantly, and Sam felt himself relax.

A blow to his right shoulder hit him so hard that he staggered and almost fell out of his chair. "What the heck was that for?" he yelled and grabbed the table for support with his other hand. Haskill grinned at him and brandished the small tube he had carried. Sam recognized the object as a microchip implanter. "You could have warned me," he growled in anguish. His arm throbbed with shooting pains that stretched down to his fingertips.

"It works better when it is a surprise, Sam. It keeps people from tensing up and helps us avoid having to repeat the procedure." Dr. Gage's voice was matter of fact, almost clinical.

Sam blinked hard and fought the black and white spots that danced before his eyes.

"Christ, Steve. How hard did you hit him?" The voice sounded very far away to Sam.

"Barely touched him, sir. Didn't think he'd be a fainter."

"I'm fine. I'm fine," Sam croaked and sat back in the chair with shaking hands. The haze cleared as the worst of the pain abated.

"Happy to hear that, Sam, because what you are about to learn may bowl you over again," Dr. Gage handed Sam a towel and waved dismissively toward Haskill. "You can leave us now, Steve. I've got the helm."

Chuckling to himself, Haskill wagged the chip implanter at Sam and departed.

Dr. Gage shook his head with indulgence and not a little irritation. "He'll get over it, Sam. But I would steer clear of him for a while yet." He slid the scanner back in front of Sam, who wiped down his face and hands. "Please touch the scanner again with your right hand."

Sam let go of his sore arm and gingerly placed his hand on the scanner. As it glowed blue, Sam felt his upper arm tingle as if it had fallen asleep. "Corporeal Security Protection?" he asked with wide eyes.

"Yes," Dr. Gage nodded, "but with some important modifications. Only chipped personnel can access the program's material when the palm scan is matched to several other biometric indicators through that device Steve just implanted. However, this particular design has an additional feature." He stood and moved closer to Sam until the latter felt his upper arm tingle again.

"It has a proximity indicator," he said flatly.

"Yes, it does. It will detect other humans within a specified radius and whether those humans are similarly chipped. An alert will fire if any protected information or materials are disclosed in the presence of an unchipped person or if the chip is tampered with or removed."

Sam tensed. "I can see now why you warned me about not being able to back out."

"Yes. But there's one more thing you should know, Sam. This specialized microchip has a language-processing technology that activates whenever its owner uses any words associated with the program and it monitors and records any and all conversations that use them. Any suspected information leaks will result in the immediate deployment of my brother's security team."

Sam took a few moments to absorb and consider his predicament. He had heard of such technology before but was not aware that it was authorized for use outside of the Nuclear and Prohibited Armaments communities. Because his role at Midgard had given his words the weight of Gage's authority, he was already careful about what he said and to whom. This, however, was an entirely new level of discretion.

He felt cold and then began to shudder. The room spun.

"I—I don't feel well, sir." The words dragged from his lips as they, along with his limbs, went numb, and he wondered if he would actually pass out this time.

"Just relax, Sam. Let the drug take effect."

Drug? Sam's increasingly sluggish thoughts fought for comprehension, and he slipped off the chair to the floor.

"Sam Richmond," Director Gage said. "Welcome to Operation Utengard."

CHAPTER NINETEEN:

OPERATION UTENGARD

Sam felt heavy, as if his body was encased in a weighted shroud, but pressure and not pain held him down. Indistinct voices prattled in the background along with the sounds of a door opening or closing. He blinked and glimpsed concrete barriers in a dimly lit space. An authoritative, feminine voice said, "He is coming around." The other sounds stilled, and the bunk on which he lay raised his upper body.

"Drink this. It will revive you," the same voice ordered. His mouth opened automatically in response to pressure on his lips. A cool, refreshing liquid trickled down his throat. Its spicy flavor reminded him of the cloves he and Tamara had once experimented with. His awareness improved, but his limbs still felt like they were tied down. He blinked hard again to bring himself into full consciousness, and as his vision cleared, his eyes landed on the most beautiful woman he had ever seen.

Am I hallucinating? The woman had unmarked, glowing pale skin and large eyes that appeared black in the low light but hinted at a lighter hue. Her facial structure was striking in its proportions, and her features were so smooth that she resembled a stress test mannequin's. *I probably look like a troll in comparison*, he thought and felt the familiar pang at the knowledge of his physical shortcomings.

She scrutinized him, and he felt a pleasant tingle of attraction that must have been mental since he couldn't control his limbs. "Wha—or who?" he mumbled; each syllable slurred. His lips and tongue, like the rest of his body, felt thick and awkward.

"Hold on, Richmond. Let your muscles recover from the effects of the soporific. The drink will help in a minute or two." Her voice was deeper than he expected. Deep, yet musical and even.

After about a minute, he felt lighter, and his fingers and toes prickled as if circulation had been restored. He wiggled them, and the woman nodded appreciatively. "See? It's working already. Here, I will help you sit up, but we will go slowly. No sudden movements. Understood?"

"Yes," he responded, and this time the word came out normally. *I know her from somewhere,* he thought, but his mind was still sluggish from the effects of the original drug. She held out her hands, and he grasped them. As he did so, he felt a warm sensation in his right arm that contrasted sharply with the coldness of her hands. The opposing temperatures made him gasp.

She frowned and gripped his hands harder. "Do you feel dizzy?"

He shook his head. "No, just disoriented." His brow furrowed. The woman was dressed in an immaculate aquamarine jumpsuit, one that Sam had only seen once before during a government demonstration at Midgard. It was the uniform of the elite diplomatic corps.

Her mouth quirked to one side at his scrutiny, a move that accentuated the dimple in her chin. "Let me know when you are ready to stand."

"I think I can manage," he said wryly. Energy returned to him rapidly, courtesy of whatever stimulant she'd given him. "You seem to know who I am, but I cannot place you." He pushed himself to a standing position.

She watched him closely and waited for him to stumble. When he did not, she crossed her arms and smiled with tight lips. "Good work standing up, Richmond. We have not met, though doubtless you've heard as much about me as I have about you. I'm Rowen Gage and," she shrugged, "I had intended that we meet under different circumstances, as did my father."

Ah, thought Sam, and relaxed. Dr. Gage's daughter. He had seen her in pictures and videos, but those images did not do her justice. "I'm—uh, glad to meet you and likewise on the circumstances." He paused. "How should I address you? Ambassador Gage? Ms. Gage?"

She raised her eyebrow in an expression so reminiscent of her father's that Sam momentarily quailed. "Well, most people here do call me 'ma'am' or 'Ambassador Gage,' but I think you and I had best use our given names with each other." When he continued to frown, she sighed impatiently. "Just call me Rowen, and I'll call you Sam instead of Richmond."

"You look too young to be an ambassador anyhow," he blurted out before his better senses stopped him. He could have kicked himself for his lack of control when her face hardened.

"And you look too young be my father's so-called left-hand man," she retorted. "If you're feeling well enough to toss out insults, you can come with me now to meet with Uncle Anton."

Uncle Anton? The title was so incongruous with Sam's perspective on the General that he sputtered. Fortunately,

Rowen was too busy setting the locking mechanism on the door to notice.

He followed her through a maze of concrete walls and rusted I-beams that housed barracks and small workstations, and they passed some dirty, exhausted people in the black, white, and gray of the General's special militia. They were rank with sweat and a chemical smell. A few of them bore scars and some had prosthetic limbs, but all of them looked well-nourished underneath their dishevelment. Rowen's cool, aqua-clad beauty made her stand out like a flower amongst ashes, and everyone they passed seemed drawn to her light.

They ascended a stairwell and into the largest operations center Sam had ever seen. The walls contained windows made of what Sam identified as an armored glass compound or something very much like it. He scanned the terrain surrounding the building and was surprised to see Midgard's latticed dome sparkling in the distance, just a few miles away.

"How long has this facility been here?" he asked Rowen as he moved toward the window and looked down. The floor they were on was at least twenty feet from the ground and should have been visible from Midgard. In fact, Sam realized, he had flown over this very spot several times with Jody and had been in its vicinity with survey and meteorology teams.

This is where that attack was supposed to have taken place from. Whoever attacked knew of this place's existence.

Rowen joined Sam at the window. "Since about three years after Midgard activated. Each operational capsule has a protection center like this one although this is the largest. And, if the people in these centers are doing their job, the capsule personnel will never know they exist." She met his eyes, and in the light, Sam saw they were a clear, pale green like the recycled glass tiles in the galley of his former home.

Her beauty was distracting, and Sam had to force himself to focus on his surroundings. He returned his attention to the window and, upon closer inspection, saw faint traces of mesh around the perimeter of the structure. "Optical netting," he mused, "with some kind of modification that projects an outer image to match the surrounding topography."

"Almost." Rowen pointed to the top of the window, where the net's ceiling was just visible. "The meshwork also emits signal inhibitors, which—"

"Which explains why the facilities do not register on our scanners," he finished for her. "And the pilots have to know of their existence."

"Exactly," she agreed. "But the pilots don't know why they exist—only that they do." She turned from the window and waved her arm for him to follow. "Come. We don't want to keep my uncle waiting."

Sam trailed in her wake while he absorbed the details of his new surroundings. People dressed in a variety of muted colors clustered around ubiquitous digital tableaus of capsules and their associated restricted areas. Sam recognized the dark urban camouflage uniforms of the Interior Police as well as the steel gray of the civil defense forces and the olive green of the military. The fact that they were all mixed together signaled an unprecedented level of cooperation between services that normally fought each other fiendishly for scarce government resources.

I wonder what common enemy—or enemies—has brought them together.

At the far end of the chamber sat a large theater-like area with terraced rows of uniformed men and women who wore visors and whispered into headsets. General Anton Gage was on the lowest level. He leaned over a large circular mockup of a geographical area Sam did not immediately recognize. As he and Rowen stepped down toward the map table, Sam saw clusters of blue and red dots clash while other similar figures zoomed across the map.

The woman to General Gage's right saw them approach and murmured into his ear. He looked up with an unreadable expression and assumed a rigid stance with his hands on his hips. Sam again felt discomfited by the contrast between his mentor's physical resemblance to this man and their polar opposite dispositions.

The General sensed Sam's unease and his eyes gleamed, but Sam could not tell if it was with pleasure or malice. He strode over to his niece. "Hello my dear. You're late, you know." His voice was rough and gravelly, as if he had been using it a great deal.

"Hello, Uncle. It's good to see you, too," Rowen responded, and undaunted, she stood on tiptoe and gave him a perfunctory kiss on the cheek. Sam saw the General's face soften, but only for a fraction of a second before the man turned an icy glare to him.

"Are you ready, Richmond?"

An echo from the past—a momentary flashback to the test proctor at the mouth of the Tunnel—unnerved him and he was momentarily dumbstruck by the comparison.

"Yes, Uncle, he's ready," Rowen answered in an exasperated voice when Sam did not respond.

"I asked him, not you," the General responded with a look that would have subdued the most hardened rebel. Rowen, however, did not seem to care, and she nodded at Sam to respond.

Sam felt his right arm warm as he strove to remain calm. "I am, sir."

"Then stop wasting time. Let's get this over with so I can get back to fighting our war." He marched up the amphitheater stairs at a pace so brisk that Sam and Rowen had to jog to keep up. They proceeded to a set of glass doors offset from rest of the open bay. As they went inside, Rowen pressed a touchscreen. The room dimmed as the illumination transitioned from white to ultraviolet light.

Rowen grabbed some visors from a wall locker and handed them out. Sam put his on and heard the General say, "Run Utengard brief, stage two."

Sam's stomach heaved as the floor underfoot turned from a flat gray sponge into a digital map of North America. He stepped on the Rocky Mountains, but his foot went through the image, and he realized he was in a virtual reality environment. Blue and red bubbles with stars and leaves on them respectively dotted the landscape. Each blue-starred dome was surrounded by oblong-shaped patterned areas. Small green squares were clustered throughout, with concentrations south of the Canadian border. Masses of red triangles lay opposite them on the northern perimeter.

"What do you see, Sam?" the General asked.

Ah. So, we're going to play a guessing game. Sam walked east toward the largest blue star. "This is Midgard," he said. "And this," he side-stepped to large yellow x just to its left, "is where the Stingray attack happened."

He looked north at the Canadian capsules and assessed the position of the red and green shapes. "Canada and the United States have forces—probably paramilitary forces—massed in border outposts."

Sam turned toward the direction of the General's voice and saw his lifelike avatar dressed in a plain black skin suit with sensors—the same type that soldiers wore underneath their exoskeleton battle suits. He looked down and saw that he was similarly clad, as was Rowen.

"Correct," the General affirmed. "Now, what do you make of these?"

Fiery bursts appeared outside the perimeters of the twenty or so American capsules whose restricted zones bordered urban population centers. The Nevada capsule, located well outside his hometown, was one of them, and Sam walked to its position to get a better look. He saw a mixture of red and purple dots outside of its restricted area. They were so densely packed together that they looked like smudges of blood.

"I presume they signify unrest, riots, terrorist, or other violent activity in the vicinity of each Capsule's restricted zone." Sam walked north into Canada and paused. "Canada appears to have far less such activity."

"Yes," Rowen agreed as she joined him. "Canada's climate is more temperate than ours, and they were more forward-looking when it came to provisioning their citizens. Although our technology far exceeds most of the Canadian Human Resiliency capabilities, our population is much more restive." Her avatar, which did not do her likeness justice, met his gaze. "The frequent attacks are disrupting our Capsule program's progress, which is nearly at a standstill. My team's current mission is to convince the Canadian government to extend their—" she hesitated and chose her next word carefully, "protection to our Capsule program in exchange for our assistance in helping them advance their own. Together we stand a chance of saving far more people than if we stand alone."

That explains why Canada would want to attract some of our people, Sam thought. But something was off. He sensed an enormous gap between what he was being told and what he had seen in his own research, and he made up his mind to find out what was missing—and why—as soon as possible.

He walked across the map to scrutinize the activity around the restricted areas, and he homed in on the Utengard facilities. After a few minutes' contemplation, he looked at the General and cleared his throat. "I didn't realize that our capsules were so—ah—exposed. Capsule intelligence showed the threat to be minimal, that is—"

"Until the Midgard attack," the General finished. "That is intentional. My job—and the sole purpose of Operation Utengard—is to protect our enclaves from outside interference so that big brains like you and my brother and your illustrious colleagues can focus on engineering successful capsule environments without... distractions."

"So," Sam said as he walked through three restricted areas, each marked with a blinking green square, "you must feed the capsule intelligence and security cells false information then."

The General held up his hand. "Not false information, Richmond. The Utengard staff sends them excellent simulated material so they can practice their skillset. Once there is no longer a significant threat, they will have access to the same intelligence feeds as everyone else. Until then, we have to protect them as well."

Sam snorted. "That's just as bad as the government 'protecting' its citizens by obscuring the truth. Propaganda is propaganda no matter what terms you use to describe it."

The General's avatar took on a menacing stance. "You've never seen war, Richmond. Otherwise, you wouldn't have such a superior attitude about the so-called truth, especially when it comes to staving off insurrection."

"Perhaps," Sam said coldly, though he quailed inside. "But I don't consider wisdom to be folly, and neither did my mother. "

The General sneered. "Your mother never fought in a war either."

"No, but she fought disease, disfigurement, and death her entire adult life." Sam was unsure how his avatar appeared, but he felt himself shake with anger. "And, like you, she didn't always win," he said as he pointed to the yellow x.

The General's avatar flexed its shoulders as if getting ready to brawl. "Careful, Richmond," he said in a low, rumbling voice that portended violence.

Before either had a chance to further escalate the disagreement, Rowen's avatar sidestepped in between them and put its hand on the General's chest. "Let's stay on topic, Uncle," she said quietly. However, her tone was threaded with steel.

Sam saw the General's chest expand and contract, as if its owner was struggling for control. The impression was one of a caged animal that raged at its bonds but was forced to accept them, if only for the moment.

Sam was unable to savor the General's discomfiture because Rowen then rounded on him. "And your attitude is not helpful either," she said scornfully.

She stepped forward and faced both of them, her arms crossed. "You two don't have to like each other but remember that we're all on the same side here. And, right now, our most pressing enemy is this." As she spoke, an image of the Doomsday clock that Sam remembered from his post-ceremony Capsule briefing appeared over the center of the map.

The palpable tension in the room lessened but only by the smallest of margins. The General's posture relaxed as he nodded at his niece, but he maintained his haughty demeanor. Sam exhaled, and the fury of the moment—along with the fear and disappointments of the past two days—gushed out of him, leaving him hollow and exhausted.

"Yes, you're right." Resigned, he turned back to the General. "What do you need me to do, General?"

The simulation suddenly turned off, and the world went black.

CHAPTER TWENTY:

THE TASK

"What I need," the General said in the darkness, "is for you to find your mother. Our lives depend on it."

The hairs on the back of Sam's neck rose up. He removed his visor and saw only the faintest outline of the General's form in dark, which caused him to shudder.

Rowen switched the dimmers back to white light and they stood looking at each other.

"You need me to find my mother." Sam's eyes were hard. "I've been trying to do just that ever since she left with no success. What makes you think that I can find her now?"

The General's next words were calm, if tinged with disdain. "Because now, courtesy of my brilliant but misguided brother, you will have access to the best information and personnel available."

When Sam remained silent, he continued, "My people tested your theory about the relationship between the disappearances and the attacks and determined that it has merit. Every Human Resiliency Program disappearance correlates with some act of violence or disruption, and the same is true for the higher-Tier disappearances." He held up a finger. "That is, with one glaring exception."

"The attack on Midgard," Sam said, grimly. "No one has gone missing yet. But—"

"The attackers botched the execution of their assault," the General finished. In response to the wariness in Sam's eyes, he added, "Stephan sent me your analysis of the attack yesterday and my people confirmed it this morning. It appears that your assessment about that was correct as well."

That's as close as I am likely to ever get to a compliment from this man, Sam thought irreverently. But he caught a grimace from Rowen and decided to keep thoughts like that to himself for the time being.

"And none of the Disappeared have been discovered in Canada, unless..." Sam could not hide his resentment, "that information, too, has been kept secret."

"Unfortunately, Sam, none of our people have turned up in Canada or elsewhere, including Dr. Richmond," Rowen said gently. "And we've used all kinds of surveillance mechanisms to find them. Trust me."

The hope that had fleetingly bloomed in Sam's gullet withered at these words. "But you believe that, with accurate information, I might be able to help you determine where our people and my mother went."

"Yes," the General confirmed. "If not, we have only one other option." He signaled to Rowen.

She hesitated and then commanded, "Run Operation Withering Leaf!"

The three of them replaced their visors, and the image that met them was one of blue arrows emanating out of the Arctic circle.

"About three years ago, the Canadian government discovered an ancient microbe buried deep in the Arctic permafrost, one that was not dangerous to the life forms of its time, which did not include humans." The General's voice was leaden. The blue arrows slowly turned red and then stopped in the northernmost area of the Northwest Territories. "It mutated shortly after its exposure to high temperatures. Even though they quarantined immediately, the team of paleontologists and geo-engineers who discovered it perished within days."

"What kind of microbe?" Sam asked, interested.

"Our information suggests it was some combination of a hantavirus and dengue fever," Rowen said, and a picture of a circular, bulbous microbe with spikes at its poles appeared, "similar to the one that ravaged England in the fifteenth and sixteenth centuries."

"So, we now have a modern form of the so-called sweating sickness on our hands." Sam wasn't sure whether to be terrified or intrigued and decided that he would have to find a balance between the two.

"We believe so, yes."

A dangerous microbe indeed, Sam thought as he examined the image with fascination. Aloud he said, "Both viruses were transmitted through animal bites—rodents for the hantavirus and mosquitoes for dengue. This is of similar construction." He looked up at Rowen and the General. "I wouldn't be so concerned if I were you. So few of either creature are left that any transmission outside of that initial outbreak is unlikely."

Rowen appraised Sam with an inscrutable expression. "Unfortunately, Sam, it mutated before it could be fully contained. We believe this new version can be transmitted via other means."

"What caused that kind of mutation?" Sam asked, puzzled, and paled when he comprehended what must have happened. "Or, should I say, whom?"

"The Canadian Human Resiliency program," the General answered promptly. "As my niece here mentioned, they need our technology badly. Their program is in danger of going under."

Again, Sam felt that something was off. He—or they—still had not fully brought him into their confidence. *And they might not ever do so,* he realized. But the thought of what had been done with the virus sickened him. "They weaponized the microbe," he said, angrily.

"Yes, Sam, they have," Rowen said, as her avatar studied the map below. "But that is not the only thing they've weaponized." She pressed her hand into the wall controller. The image of the microbe multiplied exponentially into a faint pink mist of virus-laden droplets. Sam unconsciously held his breath to prevent himself from inhaling the simulated virus. The vapor slowly started to gyrate, and, as it gained momentum, it transformed into a blackish-green vortex striped with red. The clash of colors spread across the northern United States until the entire country turned red.

Under his breath, Sam muttered, "And all it would take is a series of artificial storms—" He broke off, unwilling to put that terrible thought into words.

The General heard and finished the thought for him. "To wipe out most of the entire population south of the Canadian border? Yes. Assuming that Canada now has direct or proxy access to a storm generator or equivalent."

The simulation ended, and Sam's visor went black. *So, Canada orchestrated that attack through one of its US-based proxies.* He removed it and saw General Gage and his niece standing before him like blue ghosts in the ultraviolet light. Rowen held out a hand, and he gave her his visor as he saw the same strange light at the same time.

"What is the mortality rate?" he asked and steeled himself for the response.

"Our most conservative estimates put it at above ninety percent," she responded and busied herself with replacing the visors in the locker.

Over ninety percent. It sounded awful to the average bystander, but Sam also knew that, in a matter of decades, environmental conditions would do the same or worse to the entire world's population. Unless—

"They will need a vaccine or some genetic resiliency to the virus before they can use the weapon. That's why you need my mother. You think she would be able to help us protect ourselves from this virus, thereby eliminating the threat."

"Yes, Richmond. Exactly," the General said. "We're in an arms race with Canada to develop a mechanism that can prevent or cure this pathogen."

"That and diplomacy," Rowen added hastily. "Our core outreach team hopes to negotiate an exchange instead, without letting them know we are aware of their biological weapon. Our technology and talent for their resources, so to speak. Together we could build thousands of capable capsules in a quarter of the time it would take either of us."

"But you want the ability to use presumed immunity as a bargaining chip," Sam said flatly.

"Well, yes," Rowen said after a sideways glance at the General. "That's where you come in."

"What if I am unable to find my mother?"

"Then, Richmond, you can put your considerable talents to work finding a solution instead." The General mocked him but was serious at the same time.

Sam covered his face with his hands. *This is wrong. This is all wrong. How has it come to this?* Was this deadly game a symptom of the end of humanity or was it destined to be its root cause?

After a moment to collect himself, he removed his hands and made eye contact with the General. "I still don't see why you want me to work on the cure. Dozens of Human Engineers are far more capable of finding a defense against this—thing—than I am."

"Including your mother," Rowen reminded him.

"If I can find her. If I can't, you had better have another contingency in mind," Sam responded.

"Well, actually, Sam, we do," Rowen responded.

"Oh? Pray enlighten me."

Rowen ignored the sarcasm but shook her head in warning at her uncle, who had bristled at Sam's remark. "Did Dr. Richmond ever mention the project she was working on when she disappeared?"

"No," he admitted, though it hurt him to do so. He wondered again why she had not taken him into her confidence. "I knew about her promotion, but I distanced myself from her work so I could focus on my Accessions preparations. All of her research was seized after she left, and I was not privy to its contents."

The General crossed his arms and, with a smug expression, said, "We have her materials, Richmond. She was working on a counteractive gene sequence, and only a handful of humans out there have natural resistance. And, unlike Canada, we have access to one of them."

Tam, Sam thought. *This all comes back to her. That's how Mom got her into Capsule and why Tam wasn't downgraded after her probationary period.* It made sense, and now the rest of the puzzle fell into place. His jaw hardened.

"The Canadians wanted to get their hands on Tam—Tamara Ashraf." *And it did not matter if she was dead or alive.*

Burning anger born of a primal desire to protect her coursed through his veins, but he put it out with an icy control.

The General nodded. "Exactly."

Rowen, however, studied her feet, and Sam was confused. *She's doesn't like this option.* But that mystery would have to be solved later. He turned back to the General. "How much time do I have?"

"Our sources indicate the Canadian Human Engineers are close to a solution. We have two months. Three at most."

Sam looked to Rowen for confirmation, but she avoided his eyes. "That isn't much time."

"I expect that your genius can compensate for the time constraint," the General remarked sardonically, "and that you can manage this task in between your training requirements."

"Training?" Sam asked, surprised. "What training?"

"I know you can think, Richmond," the General admitted as if it pained him to do so. "What you can't do is fight, and that is a critical weakness. Therefore, you will train, and you will fight like everyone else in Utengard. That is," he mused, looking at Rowen, "when you are not working on your assigned tasks."

The General's wristlet buzzed. "I have to get back to the operations center," he said. "Rowen will take you to one of the bunkers so you can change. I suggest you begin your search by determining who initiated the Midgard attack and what they wanted." The General handed his visor to Rowen.

"Yes, sir," Sam responded tightly. He fought back the childish urge to spit at the man.

"Oh, and one more thing," General Gage added over his shoulder. "Understand this. I don't like you or trust you, and only my brother's recommendation got you here. But I make all of the decisions at Utengard, and while here, you answer to me and my lieutenants, not his. I don't care if my brother offers you the command of a capsule tomorrow. You now work for me until I decide otherwise."

"I understand," Sam responded with clenched fists.

"I understand, *sir*," General Gage corrected severely. He scanned Sam's reedy frame and pallor, and his face assumed a predatory appearance. "I'll see you on the training grounds, Richmond."

CHAPTER TWENTY-ONE:

THE DRONE

One month later

Sam felt like he was drowning in his own perspiration. Rivulets of sweat trickled down his neck, back, and buttocks, and globules dribbled from his hair into his eyes, blinding him. His legs and arms shook with the effort of sprinting over undulating terrain. Cramps in his midsection prevented him from standing upright, even in the stiff exoskeleton of his battle suit, and the oxygen he inhaled likewise provided little relief.

"Physical endurance levels reaching critical. Three minutes, twenty-two seconds to collapse." The voice of Troy, his monitor—the human responsible for reading his battle suit's output and tracking the situation from afar—piped through his helmet's speakers in an annoyingly cheerful tone. "Enemy ground forces are one kilometer and closing."

"Right," Sam gasped, too exhausted to be snappish. "Options?"

"Remaining options are: conceal in place, replenish, pulse, and—"

"What… about… a drone swarm?" Sam interrupted in between breaths.

"Negative," the monitor responded. "Friendly forces too close in proximity."

"How long to replenish?"

"Two minutes, forty-five seconds."

"Fuck!" Sam cursed, frustrated.

"No time for that kind of activity now, Richmond," Troy quipped. "Three minutes to shut down, enemy approaching."

A static buzzing filled Sam's ears. For a second, he thought it was a precursor to losing consciousness. But the unmistakable movements of enemy battle suit pulses as several of them moved through the layers of dead brush to his left convinced him otherwise. Damage he sustained earlier in the battle had severed the quantum communications link with his team, and he was not certain about their exact location.

"Recommendations?" he panted. More static followed the pause. *Damn him!* Troy was not especially creative in tight spots like this one; Sam was by far the better innovator. In fact, he often thought their roles should have been reversed. He would have had several alternatives prepared by now.

"Change of plans." Sam paused to catch his breath. "Deploy single microdrone in vicinity of enemy eastern flank."

"What? That won't even—"

"Just do it and notify the friendlies!" Sam commanded.

"Yes, sir." Troy's response was subdued. A panel opened in the backside of Sam's battle suit, and he caught a glimpse of the tiny drone—which was no larger than an insect—as it flashed to life and headed eastward.

"Action complete," Troy continued. "But you must replenish within the next two minutes."

"Fine. Replenish now," Sam ordered and lay down. Through the reflective visor on his helmet, the sky looked like a beige desert wasteland in which the clouds served as dunes. His battle suit warmed, and he felt weight shift from the solar energy stores in the backpack to the vein-like wires of the exoskeleton. *Too bad my physical energy reserves cannot be so easily restored.*

An explosion followed by a series of shouts to the east made Sam smile. His little drone had made it to its intended target. Sam prayed it had caused some serious damage when it self-destructed.

Juneau, Sam's combat trainer, had suggested that he concentrate on drone skills to compensate for his lack of prowess in short-range warfare, and Sam subsequently experimented with both formation flying and individual Unmanned Aerial Vehicle (UAV) maneuvers. His teammates were skeptical about the impact of the latter, but Sam rationalized that someone would have to test the theory, so it might as well be him. *If I was right and my drone ruse worked, I just might make it through this battle alive and, when I do, I will finally be able to—*

"Enemy closing on your position!" The panic in Troy's voice was tangible.

"Evasive—" Sam began but, before he could complete the command, the shadow of an enemy battle suit loomed over him, its rifle pointed directly at his face. He held his breath and waited for the blow, and he was not disappointed. His entire battle suit shook violently as a husky voice exulted, "You're dead, Richmond."

Sam closed his eyes. *Damn! I was so close this time.* "Conceded," he grumbled through gritted teeth. "Should I sit out the rest of the exercise here or head back to base?"

"I bet you wish you could stay here and take a nap. Don't you?" Juneau held out a heavily armored hand and, before Sam could retort, hauled him to his feet with a hook-shaped tool. "Now, remind me how many times you've died this week, Richmond?"

As the head of the Opposing Forces or OPFOR for the training exercises, Juneau kept a tally of everyone's performance, and he was amused at the frequency with which Sam was killed in action. However, Sam knew he was at risk of washing out of the program—and increasing General Gage's already substantial ire—if his results did not improve.

"Only three times this week," Sam retorted with humor. He knew better than to show his frustration; his squad mates were relentless practical jokers who would rib him mercilessly if he did otherwise. They, like most of the Utengard forces, used humor as a shield against the stark reality of their mission.

"Well, that's an improvement at least," Juneau said lightly. "Anyhow, a message came just now. The General wants to see you this afternoon, and I have orders to take you back to headquarters."

Despite the heat, Sam felt chilled. *This is not good.* "What about the rest of this exercise?"

"Uh, you're dead, Richmond. Remember?"

"Right, but the rules stipulate we're supposed to stay until the after-action review concludes."

Juneau stomped forward in his battle suit and would have shrugged had its bulk allowed. "General's orders take precedence. But you're right. I need to let them know you're leaving." He turned toward the sound of a crash through the deadfall. "Speak of the devil," he remarked when a man in a battle suit that matched Sam's joined them in the clearing. "Ember," Juneau called to Sam's squad leader, "Release Richmond and mark him down as KIA. Give his monitor a break, too. I expect he needs one."

Ha! That unoriginal automaton needs a permanent break, and the sooner the better. Sam was out of patience with Troy, especially after the day's events.

"Roger," Ember responded and then pounded his battle suit's hand on the shoulder of Sam's. "By the way, Richmond, nice job, except for getting yourself killed again. The single drone idea almost worked. I'd like to take a look at your UAV training regimen once we finish up here."

"Of course," Sam responded and felt the warm glow of Ember's praise. Despite his constant mistakes and lack of something they called "killer instinct," Sam had a good relationship with the members of his squad. They accepted him, flaws and all, as one of their own, and Sam recognized the unfamiliar feeling he had around them as camaraderie. "At least I was helpful in one respect this time."

Juneau chuckled. "You know, you almost had us with that little maneuver. In fact, if the OPFOR team had been looking in any other direction, that drone of yours might have done more damage. Unfortunately, for you, we saw it, which alerted us to the fact that you were still a viable target and out there all alone. An interesting idea, though."

"Thanks. I hope the General shares your assessment of my doctrinal deviancy."

"Hard to tell with him," Juneau mused. He and Sam waved a farewell to Ember and made their way to the battle suit bay at the edge of the training grounds. They deactivated the suits and stowed them in their assigned charging stations. Sam gagged at the odor that emanated from his under-tunic, the result of several days in the field. "Hey, do I have time to clean up before we head out?"

"No, but I wouldn't worry about it. It will give the General the impression that you are working hard," Juneau joked.

Sam shook his head and joined him in a Goshawk covered in camouflage radar-resistant paint. "Mind if I drive, Richmond?"

Sam broke out in a self-deprecating smile. "I see that my reputation precedes me."

"Yup, none of us can escape our successes or failures. Our mission is too important. And you're even more special than the rest of us."

Juneau spoke the words without rancor, but a shadow crossed Sam's face. Once—just once—he wanted to be normal, ordinary, or any other condition that would allow him to avoid notice rather than attract it.

The Goshawk hovered over the docking station and then veered to the Southeast. Juneau put the encrypted directions into the system navigator. He looked sideways at Sam, whose face registered his many concerns. "You know, Richmond, General Gage is hard on all of us. But he knows what he's doing. Every person in Utengard trusts him with their lives."

Sam nodded slowly, "I've seen that." It was true. The man did inspire incredible loyalty. He was demanding but fair, and he was not afraid to make tough decisions. However, Sam remained unable to shake his sense of unease whenever he was in the General's presence. Something about him was dark and ruthless but also strangely familiar, and Sam suspected some of his anxiety stemmed from the unknown source of the familiarity. But no one else seemed to share Sam's discomfort. "I guess I just haven't worked with him as long as the rest of you."

"No, but you always seem more nervous around him with each encounter, not less."

Sam sighed and covered his face with his hands. "I'm tired and stressed. That's all. The pressure is on, and I haven't been able to deliver."

Juneau received a signal that he was departing a controlled area, and he put the Goshawk into stealth mode. "That's understandable, but you know you can always count on me and the team for help." Concern filled his eyes as he observed Sam's dishevelment. "When was the last time you slept?"

"I can't remember," Sam mumbled and shook himself.

"See? That's at least one thing I can help you with. Take a little siesta, Richmond. I'll wake you up if and when I need you."

"Thanks," Sam said, and though it felt uncomfortable to accept help, the invitation was welcome. He closed his eyes. *At least I'm not bored anymore.* Quite the opposite, in fact. He was exhausted. Between training exercises, combatives practice, and time spent at the research station, he barely had time to breathe, let alone rest.

But sleep eluded him. He suspected General Gage wanted a progress report, and he had not yet decided which information to reveal… or conceal. Anton Gage demanded results, and Sam knew he could produce them, but he was leery about putting everything he had discovered on the table with anyone, let alone that man. The challenge was that, unlike his brother, the General was a human lie detector who would not hesitate to hurt anyone who deceived him regardless of their value. Therefore, a strategy of omission carried risk, but it was a far less perilous option than subterfuge.

I've obscured the most important findings, Sam reminded himself. He suspected that his research and related activities were monitored, and he spent his first days at the Utengard headquarters finding and subverting their physical and digital surveillance systems. He devoted two additional days to the development and employment of digital countersurveillance algorithms so they would see him progress, but not nearly as far—or as deep—as he actually proceeded.

He had discovered the principal organization responsible for the attacks, even though their sponsors remained elusive, and he had figured out how their storm generation technology functioned. But he was no closer to finding the source or destination of the Disappeared. That, at least, was one thing he could be completely open about.

I'll worry about that later, Sam thought, drained. This flight was the first time Sam had even sat down in quite a while, and he stopped fighting for awareness. Within minutes, the smooth motion of the Goshawk lulled him to sleep.

* * *

It was not the deep, dreamless sleep that his body needed for recovery. Instead, Sam was back in the cavern with the strange man with the cropped gray hair, but now both of them wore battle suits. This time, he anticipated the man's aggression, and he fought back. They grappled on the cave's rocky floor, but the man in black was the more proficient fighter. Soon, he had Sam on his stomach, arms pinned from behind. Bizarrely, Sam's attention was less on his compromising position and more on the composition of the rocks his face was smashed against. He recognized volcanic tuff and layers of carbonate and sediment.

The faceless voice spoke again, but more urgently. "You must make your choice, Sam, and soon. One path is mapped but will take you to certain death. The other is hidden but leads to life."

"I'm pinned down!" Sam cried.

"And there you will stay," the faceless man responded as he manipulated Sam's arms and pressed his face harder into the cave floor. Sam choked, unable to breathe. *Here I die.*

A sudden movement resulted in the complete release of pressure. When Sam rolled over, he saw another person in a battle suit had thrown the faceless man against the wall.

Sam's savior removed its helmet and revealed the care-worn face of a man in his late forties with a star-shaped scar on his left cheek. He was half bald, and the other half of his scalp was full of long, black hair streaked with white.

"Who are you?" Sam asked.

Instead of responding, the scarred man stepped out of his suit and held a hand to Sam. "Come with me, Samuel Richmond," he said. "I will show you where to find her."

Sam followed him to the edge of the cavern. "Follow the drone," he said. Sam felt his battle suit's pack open and release a single drone. It hovered in front of him and then raised up and glinted with a silvery, metallic sheen in the sunlight unlike any drone Sam had ever seen. He followed it with his eyes until it disappeared into the setting sun. He turned to ask the man where it was going and—

"Richmond. Richmond! Wake up!" Juneau's voice and the Goshawk's jagged movements dragged Sam out of the dream. The sky was dark, and, for a moment, Sam thought they had flown into the night. Juneau's efforts to control the Goshawk, which staggered in the face of strong winds, alerted him to the weather monitor.

"Electric storm," Juneau said. "I need some help steering and navigating."

"Roger. I've got hands on now."

For the next several minutes, Juneau and Sam communicated in single word messages as they fought against the weather that felt like its sole mission was to destroy them. They dodged electrostatic fields and narrowly avoided contact with other aircraft who were unaware of the Goshawk's presence. After an eternity, an intermittent voice broke through the static of the dormant communications system.

"Goshawk one seven, this is Utengard zero one. You have entered the Midgard exclusion zone. Acknowledge and verify identity."

Relieved, Juneau said, "It's about time, Winnie. We've been fighting through this weather for ages now. Identify verification is Juneau, Robert H., identifier seven-oh-one-oh-seven."

"Acknowledged. You are cleared to land." The specialized optical netting parted like a curtain, and Sam saw the Utengard's headquarters building appear in the middle of the simulated landscape in Midgard's restricted zone. Once inside its protective sphere, the winds stopped, and Sam realized he was panting with the exertion of flying through the storm.

As they landed, an alert beeped on Juneau's wristlet. He looked at it and frowned.

"What is it?" Sam asked.

Juneau held his breath as he considered how to respond. "I'm not sure exactly. Apparently, there was another incident, but they didn't send the details." He scrutinized Sam before he returned to the task of docking the aircraft. "You have orders to report to General Gage immediately."

Sam swallowed. "Where is he?"

Juneau opened the hatch, jumped to the ramp, and held out his hands to brace Sam in the event that he lost his balance—a frequent occurrence. "He's in the arboretum." He was unable to meet Sam's eyes. "I'm headed to the galley for some chow. I'll grab some for you."

Sam followed him down the ramp. "Juneau, wait. Where should I meet you to coordinate our return trip?" Juneau hesitated and then continued into the building. "Hey, we have to be back tonight to prep for the urban infiltration exercise tomorrow. Right?"

Juneau stopped and turned around to face Sam. "I wouldn't be so sure about that."

CHAPTER TWENTY-TWO:

THE ROSES

The Utengard staff stopped and stared at Sam as he mounted the walkway that led from the headquarters building to the arboretum. Some wrinkled their noses and, had he not been so keyed up about the unknown incident, he would have been embarrassed by his pungency. The guards outside of the arboretum eyed him with suspicion, and his apprehension increased.

The sight of the arboretum never failed to take his breath away, no matter how stressed he felt. The reinforced, triangle-paned glass glistened in the hazy sunlight. The spectacle was aided by artificial bulbs that simulated the additional light needed to sustain the wondrous selection of plants and shrubs inside. Long rows of herbs and vegetables reminiscent of capsule experiments stretched out before him, and he felt a sudden pang of longing for Tamara. She would have shared his amazement at the both the health and volume of the vegetation.

This food, however, was reserved exclusively for Utengard personnel. Sam's first meals at the headquarters had been a revelation, and the comparative health of his new colleagues and fellow soldiers now made sense. He credited his own improved mental energy and physical endurance in part to the extraordinary meals of whole, unprocessed produce that he enjoyed when at the headquarters.

The marvel of fresh herbs and vegetables, however, was nothing compared to the flowers. Their powerful, almost overwhelming fragrance was intoxicating, but the abundance of such colorful luxury momentarily overloaded his senses and made him feel dizzy. He took a moment to store the vista in his memory; his exposure to such wonders would be minimal once he returned to his assigned training area and, eventually, to Midgard to complete his life sentence in a far sparser environment.

So engrossed was he in these thoughts that he nearly ran into General Gage when he rounded a flowering tree. The dull colors of the General's urban camouflage uniform made him seem like a shadow or trick of the lighting, and only his movements alerted Sam to his presence.

The General was tending a row of flowering bushes with an odd, spiked instrument in his gloved hands. Sam watched in fascinated horror as the General used the tool to claw at the soil and lift up perfectly healthy-looking plants by the roots. So taboo was this activity—everyone knew that all green life must be preserved to reduce carbon emissions—that Sam tasted bile in his mouth and gagged.

"Are you familiar with this flower, Richmond?" the General asked without looking up.

Sam swallowed convulsively but forced himself to move closer so he could assess the plant. The flowers had huge thorns that spiked the sides of each branch. Waxy leaves in poison green sprung from amongst the thorns along with vivid, fragrant blooms the color of arterial blood. It seemed almost too perfect to be real. "I believe so, sir," he said.

"You think or you know?" The General's flinty eyes met Sam's murky green ones.

"I know, sir." Sam bit his lip. General Gage was in what Sam privately called his "interrogation mode," the one that aimed to make even the most assured victim feel clumsy, useless, or both. "They're roses."

"Hmmph. They are, indeed, roses. A special breed, in fact," the General said coldly. "This arboretum is one of only three in the country authorized to grow flowers with little nutritional or medicinal value. These—" he gestured to the plant with his spiked instrument, "used to be grown for decoration, though rose hips have anti-inflammatory qualities when appropriately curated." He returned his attention to the bush and continued to rip out the greenery near its base.

"We have healthy soil here," the General added. "So healthy that weeds flourish and will choke out the roses if left to grow. In these smaller beds, weeds compete with other plants for water, food, light, and other essential resources for life. They must be removed to preserve the health of the roses."

"So, it is beneficial, then, to kill those plants to preserve the lives of the others." Sam did not ask about the criteria a plant must meet before it was allowed to live because he knew he would not like the General's probable answer.

"Exactly, Richmond." The General's eyes bore into Sam like drills. "Come closer. I want to show you something else about caring for these delicate flowers."

The last thing he wanted to do was to move closer to General Gage, but he had no recourse. He gingerly stepped forward but kept the maximum distance possible between him and the General.

"This," the General pointed to a bloom that was completely open with petals tipped with brown, "is a blossom that will die in a matter of days—a completely normal occurrence. And these..." he pointed to compressed petals encased in light green cocoons underneath the wilting flower, "are new buds. Now, what we have to do is remove the old blooms so that these new buds can come up and flourish. The process is called dead-heading, interestingly enough." As he spoke, he placed his thumb and forefinger around the base of the overblown rose and yanked off its head.

Sam winced as General Gage did likewise with other unfortunate blossoms but forced himself to watch.

"I understand you've made little progress thus far with the Disappeared or your mother's research."

Sam felt himself grow cold, and he temporarily forgot about the sacrilegious plant executions.

He squared his shoulders. "Yes, sir, that is true. But I have made some other, perhaps more critical revelations."

General Gage stopped mid-decapitation and stared at Sam. "About what, exactly?"

"About who was responsible for the Midgard attack and how they built a storm generator." The words came out nonchalantly enough, but Sam trembled.

Slowly, the General stood until he towered over Sam while he considered the implications of that statement. He was curious about what Sam had discovered but furious that he and his people had been fooled by whatever countersurveillance mechanisms the young man before him had put in place.

And it was all Sam could do not to cringe under that piercing gaze as the General mulled over his options in silence.

"Hmmm," he murmured finally. As his lips twitched, he pressed them tightly together to prevent a smile from escaping. "Impressive, Richmond. Impressive but risky. I'm not sure whether such a clever deception warrants a punishment or reward."

Sam quailed internally, but he knew he was too valuable to kill. However, he hoped to avoid several unpleasant alternatives just short of death. "I still don't have a complete picture, though, sir," he began in the hopes that his ignorance of the facts might deter the General from prematurely dead heading him. "If you want a complete picture, I need complete and accurate information to work with. The intelligence and reports and data I've accessed are full of holes and inconsistencies."

It was on the tip of his tongue to remind the General that his attempt to deceive Sam was both problematic and needless, but he saw rage flicker in the depths of that flinty stare and decided against it.

"When did you figure that out, Richmond?"

"On my first day at Utengard," Sam admitted. The trembling in his limbs ceased as frustration overtook his nerves, and he struggled to keep his voice level. "You said you did not trust me, and I took you at your word. The gaps and conflicting information, therefore, made total sense."

The General narrowed his eyes, which now glinted with interest instead of fury. "Hmph. It appears both my brother's praise and my mistrust were warranted," he said coolly. The spiked tool he brandished in his hand might as well have been a weapon. For a moment, Sam had the bizarre thought that General Gage could and would take him out then and there. But he returned to his task of pulling up weeds and plucking off heads, though with far more vigor.

"Canada was responsible for the Midgard attack," he said. "My people determined that weeks ago."

"That's only part of the story, though, sir," Sam said cautiously as he dodged the dead buds that flew in his direction.

"Oh?" the General responded without looking up. "Astonish me."

Sam swallowed. *Here we go,* he thought. "It is true that some current or former Canadian paramilitary forces perpetrated the initial attack, but they were acting as a proxy for someone else."

General Gage paused for a split second and then continued his work on the roses. "Who were they working for?"

"I don't know for certain, sir." *Which is true.* He held on to that thought tightly as the General turned his head to the side and gave him a look so searing that Sam felt like his brain was being scraped.

"But you have your suspicions." It was a statement not a question.

"Yes, sir. Whoever is responsible is based in the United States, and they had help from someone inside the Human Resiliency Program."

"I know they had help from the inside, Richmond," the General said in a voice dripping with contempt. "That much is obvious. What I need to know is the source of these attacks and how the hell they got their hands on storm generation technology."

Sam took a deep breath and then spoke slowly and clearly. "The attacks appear to be conducted mainly by Canadian paramilitary at Midgard and at our northern border, but the others were organized by a variety of domestic groups. I suspect they, too, are proxies for a larger or broader organization. However," Sam forced himself to make eye contact with the General, "I have not yet identified the umbrella group they answer to."

"So, you haven't figured out anything of relevance then."

"It depends on what you consider relevant. I've seen strong indications that the same group hired all of the insurgent, terrorist, and paramilitary organizations, or at least they all come back to the same individual or group of individuals. Whoever they are, they are more powerful and well-resourced than even I anticipated."

General Gage waved his entrenching tool like a pointer. "Explain."

Sam took a moment to figure out how he could best articulate his strange discoveries. "The person—or persons—behind these events recruited indigent and vagrants with the right backgrounds to construct a storm generator, and possibly more than one. And they need rare earth minerals that are only available in Wyoming and Canada to do so. My models also suggest that the precision of that technology is satellite-based, but they must have the connections to keep that satellite secret."

"So," the General mused, "they have help from our government—or someone else's."

Sam nodded. "Yes, sir. Canada is a likely candidate."

"Which group do you suspect is behind this?"

"I don't know if it is a group or person, but they answer to the codename of something that comes up as 'wailing phantom' or 'screaming ghoul' or 'tortured ghost' depending on how I adjust my decryption algorithm."

General Gage absently crushed the perfectly healthy bloom in his hand as his face drained of color. "The Banshee," he said in a voice choked with raw emotion.

Comprehension dawned on Sam. "Yes, sir, that's likely. You know of them?"

"It's not a 'them,' Richmond. It's a 'he,' and he's supposed to be dead." The General turned away and paced down the line of roses while Sam watched. *He knows who this "Banshee" person is,* Sam realized. *And it's personal.*

When he returned to Sam's position, the General's voice was deadly quiet. "How certain are you of that assessment, Richmond?"

"I'm as certain as I can be given the quality of the information I have available."

"Watch it, Richmond." The threat was clear. After he composed himself, the General continued. "You've informed my brother of your findings?"

"No, sir," he said. *Of course I didn't. I don't have a death wish.* "I expected you would want to review my work and inform him yourself."

"And you've told no one else?"

"No, sir," Sam said, still confused.

When Sam bit his lip and provided additional details, the General continued. "You haven't asked me why I summoned you here today." His voice was deadly quiet.

"I presumed it was for a progress report," Sam said with foreboding.

The General grunted and waved his hand in a dismissive gesture. "I don't need to fly you out of your training exercise for a simple status report, although it appears I'll have to do a better job of monitoring your work." He paused and looked sideways at Sam. "I want to know why you vouched for your romantic rival before you left Midgard."

Sam was caught by surprise. "You mean you brought me here to talk about Hector?"

"Yes," the General said shortly. "You see, Mr. Ramirez has just gone missing, right under my brilliant brother's nose. Stephan is understandably livid, as Mr. Ramirez was part of his inner circle and could compromise our entire operation if what he knows falls into the wrong hands. I share that sentiment. Given your close personal relationship with Mr. Ramirez, I thought you might shed some light on the matter."

Hector disappeared? The shock was so great that Sam wondered whether the General's eyes had turned him to stone. "He—that is—we haven't been in contact since I left for Utengard. I don't know where he is or where might have gone."

"Oh, I know that. All of your communications are monitored. You've ignored all of his messages, not that much was in them. I'm just surprised that someone with your capabilities didn't see his departure coming."

Sam wanted to retort that he hadn't seen his own mother's disappearance coming either but thought better of it. "I can hardly believe it myself, sir," he said instead.

The General considered him for a moment. "So you say. But I know you're still hiding something from me, Richmond." He stepped into Sam's personal space and looked down on him. "Bottom line—if you want to earn my trust and keep my brother's, you need to help us find the Disappeared, starting with your mother."

"I'm trying to do that, sir, but it is a difficult task with my hands tied."

"Try harder then. Speaking of tying hands, though—" The General signaled to the arboretum's door keeper. The sliding door opened and two of General Gage's personal security detail entered. Sam's stomach dropped as they cuffed him.

"Take him to Interrogation Room Two," he ordered. The soldiers stepped forward and each took one of Sam's arms.

The General removed his gardening gloves with careful deliberation as he towered over Sam, who had paled. "I will find out what you're hiding, Richmond, even if it means destroying you and everyone you care about."

CHAPTER TWENTY-THREE:

THE TABLE

The bright white lights that illuminated the room temporarily blinded Sam after the darkness of the underground tunnel that led to the interrogation chambers. He did not struggle as the soldiers strapped him to the Table—a rectangular slab that, from a distance, had the black, metallic sheen of solar panels. Instead of silicon semiconductors, though, its surface was laden with tiny veins of sliver wire that projected energy rather than stored it. And that projected energy translated to pain for the Table's captives. Sam silently prayed for the fortitude to make it through the ordeal without inadvertently disclosing his most critical discoveries or causing harm to the woman he loved.

The truth was that Hector's disappearance threw a wrench in every theory he had about the attackers, the disappearances, and who was behind them. And Sam was angry—not at General Gage—but at Hector. Hector had befriended Sam, stolen the woman he loved, wormed his way into Dr. Gage's favor, and then turned traitor. *And if the attackers wanted Hector and not Tamara, the whole argument about a deadly weapon and its cure did not hold.* If the Banshee—whoever he was—had wanted Hector, neither he nor the Canadians he hired needed Tamara's genes.

Either they already have a counter to that pathogen, or they never weaponized it in the first place. But why, then, would the Gages believe someone had? And who was the elusive Banshee?

But Sam knew he had a limited window in which to solve those puzzles before the General and his minions started a campaign against the wrong individuals, groups, or countries. Sam wouldn't wish that on anyone.

As if to emphasize that point, two people clad in the deep burgundy of Utengard's interrogators arrived. Their suits made bloody bits of color in the otherwise stark room. Behind them was the dark, mirrored surface of one-sided glass that made Sam feel as if he faced four inquisitors instead of only two. *Three, actually,* he realized with a shudder. General Gage was most likely on the other side of the mirror; and Sam knew he was the type of person who preferred to let others ask the questions so he could listen, observe, and assess. *But he relishes the experience, too.*

The male interrogator reviewed some material on a tablet in his hands. After a few minutes, he met Sam's eyes. "Samuel J. Richmond?"

"Yes, that's me," Sam quipped.

"I am Agent Tomás Quentin. Your reputation precedes you, Mr. Richmond." He tapped in some notes on his tablet. His tone was professional, almost clinical. Without looking up, he said, "I assume you are familiar with our methods?"

Sam forced himself to appear dispassionate. "Yes. You ask me questions, and if you like the answers, we move to the next question. If you don't like what I tell you, you shock me until you hear something that pleases you."

"Almost." Agent Quentin smiled. "We will enact a reprimand, and it will not be pleasant, but we have no desire to harm the bodies or nervous systems of our... ah... guests." He gestured toward his partner, a bulky woman with short, iron-gray hair, small eyes, and masculine features. "This is Agent Marlow, our Table specialist. Ms. Marlow, please demonstrate the Table's capabilities to Mr. Richmond."

Agent Marlow placed her thumb on the base of the black metal rod she held. A tingling sensation started in the base of Sam's spine and spread outward toward his limbs. It neither hurt nor burned; rather it itched and was all the more uncomfortable because he was unable to scratch.

At a sign from Agent Quentin, Marlow lowered the device, and Sam's discomfort subsided. The Table, however, still felt warm from its exertions. "That was the lowest setting, Mr. Richmond."

"I understand," Sam said and prayed that he could get to the crux of the matter as quickly as possible. He was familiar with the Table's mechanics from his rotation with Midgard's security branch, and he knew that its minute, tailored electric shocks targeted pressure points that would not leave any lasting physical damage. However, the scale of pain it could inflict ranged from the mild prickle he had just experienced to the agonizing pain of severe burns, which frequently left its victims with significant emotional scars.

"Then let us proceed." Agent Quentin stepped closer to Sam. "Tell us, please, how you were first introduced to Hector Ramirez."

Sam caught himself before he actually rolled his eyes. "Why don't we skip over the formalities? You don't need me to reiterate information you already have from my records, so I'll save you the trouble. I don't know why Hector left or where he went. If I did know, I would have found my moth—"

The black rod hovered in the air before Sam finished speaking and, at the word "mother," the Table warmed again. This time Sam felt like he had broken out in horrible, itching hives all over his body, and he writhed with discomfort.

Agent Quentin watched him struggle with narrowed eyes until sweat broke out on Sam's forehead. He signaled to Marlow, and Sam's muscles relaxed but still felt tender. Sam watched as Agent Marlow touched his left ear, but he removed it as soon as he saw the direction of Sam's attention.

Grimly, Sam realized that he was right about who really controlled this interrogation, and it wasn't Agent Quentin.

"If I were you, I would stick to answering the questions, Mr. Richmond.But," he said as he put the tablet down, "you're right. We need not waste our time." He stepped closer to the Table. "What indications did you have that Mr. Ramirez intended to leave?"

None, Sam almost snapped. But he took time to review his final interactions with Hector in the clinic and realized he had missed some signs at the time, one in particular. Aloud, he said, "Hector asked me to take care of Tamara—Tamara Ashraf, his fiancée, in the clinic on the night after their transport was attacked. That was the last time I had contact with him." To his dismay, tears welled in his eyes. Angry tears. Hector had left Tam—who loved him—when she was at her most vulnerable, and now she, too, was under increased pressure and, quite probably, pain.

Agent Quentin, who watched Sam closely for any emotion, pressed the point. "So, Ms. Ashraf's rejection hurt you. Why, then, were you so eager to endorse the Director's choice of Mr. Ramirez as your replacement at Midgard?"

"Look, I thought Hector was a good fit for my old assistant position, even though I was jealous of his success," Sam admitted. The words tasted bitter on his lips, but he had no reason to hide that part of the truth at least. "And endorsed implies the move had my seal of approval. It did not. Dr. Gage personally selected Hector Ramirez as my replacement. Don discussed the switch the morning I left for Utengard, and I did not disagree. Can we just get past this issue and focus on finding him together instead of this nonsense?"

Frustration and ire so racked Sam that it was a full five seconds before he sensed hordes of tiny insects—or what felt very much like them—crawling all over his skin. He moved to swat the invisible creatures away, but the restraints prevented him, and he made animal sounds in the back of his throat.

The minutes spent on the Table's next higher intensity felt like hours as Sam thrashed and writhed and groaned. When Agent Marlow finally released him, Sam's entire body continued to thrum and ache with his nerves' distress.

"I strongly encourage you to be more temperate in your answers, Mr. Richmond." Agent Quentin's tone was detached, as if he was indifferent now to such sufferings.

Sam glared at him. "Torture will not give me knowledge I do not have. At best, it will only force me to tell you things that are only partially true. I can help you if you let me, without all of this drama."

The silence that followed was interrupted by a faint noise of static that emanated from Agent Quentin's head. Sam closed his eyes the better to listen. *He's waiting for instructions from the General, probably from an earpiece.*

"Very well, Mr. Richmond," Quentin purred after a few moments. "Go ahead."

Sam took a deep breath and closed his eyes to still his body and mind. "I would like to review some of the footage of Mr. Ramirez and—and my mother in the months leading up to their departures." When a stunned silence ensued, he added, "It would be easier for me to assist you from behind a terminal than from the top of this thing." He indicated the Table with a jerk of his head.

Another pause. "I'm afraid that's not possible, Mr. Richmond. However," he motioned to Agent Marlow, "we can bring the footage here and peruse it together."

Agent Marlow left then, and Sam breathed a sigh of relief at his temporary reprieve. Quentin pressed a button on the Table, and it raised up Sam's upper body like one of the clinic's beds. Optical netting lowered from the ceiling and the lights dimmed while Quentin gave Sam sidelong looks whenever his earpiece buzzed.

Marlow returned with a mobile terminal and set it up so that it faced the mirrored glass. "Very well, Richmond," Quentin commented. "When would you like to start?"

Over the next two hours, Sam scrutinized the footage of his mother and Hector. They started in the year prior to Miranda's disappearance and continued through Sam—and Hector's—arrival at their respective capsules. At first, Sam detected no anomalies and answered his inquisitors' questions as fully as he was able, knowing little was there that he had any incentive to obscure. One unforeseen difficulty was that the ubiquitous surveillance sensors and cameras did not cover private quarters for the higher-ranking personnel in the Human Resiliency Program, meaning both Miranda's and Hector's activities had significant gaps. But Sam could not shake the feeling that some vital clue was there for him alone to discover.

He had almost given up to exhaustion when an image from the Phoenix capsule archives caught his attention. "Wait!" he shouted. "Go back to that previous picture."

The excitement in his voice roused his interrogators to action. "What is it, Mr. Richmond?"

"Zoom in on that Falconet—the one docked on Phoenix's south side."

Quentin nodded. "Yes, here it is."

Sam's mouth opened in shock, but he shut it again, unwilling to commit to the theory until he reviewed more recorded activities. Instead, he said, "I didn't realize Hector and Jody knew each other."

"Jody?" Quentin asked.

"Jody Escobar. She was a pilot and pilot instructor at Midgard. Look—" unable to raise his hand he pointed with his nose, "the two of them just got out of the same cockpit."

While Quentin was distracted by running down Jody Escobar's flight records from August, Sam looked closely at the picture. *I've seen that before,* he thought. *I would just need to change the orientation of the photo and—*

"We've confirmed that Mr. Ramirez and Ms. Escobar flew three familiarization flights together in July and August of this year," Quentin interrupted. "What is the significance?"

"I'm not sure yet," Sam responded, suppressing his excitement. "I need to see more footage. Let's look at both of them in the days leading up to the Midgard attack."

Marlow continued to feed him video and still photos from the terminal. "Wait!" Sam cried. "Can you freeze that frame and zoom in on Hector's face?" However, he didn't want to see Hector's face.

Quentin signaled to Marlow, and Sam had a closer view of the video, which showed Hector, Tamara, and Sam in Midgard's clinic the evening of the attack.

There it is, he realized. It had been right in front of him from the beginning, but so blinded had he been by his preoccupation with his Midgard duties and dreams of his future with Tamara that he had missed it. The same symbol he had seen over and over again in his dreams and in life since the day his mother disappeared. But it was not something he was prepared to share—yet. Quickly, he came up with a diversion—one that would touch on the truth but leave him space and time—to fully understand.

"What is it, Mr. Richmond? What do you see?"

Damn. Once again, his face had betrayed him. His thoughts were often too transparent. "I'm not sure yet," he stalled. "I need to see frames of Hector Ramirez and Jody Escobar together from the time of that last video until the day of the attack."

While the images played, Sam feigned intense interest while his mind worked at lightspeed to develop a deterrent. He settled on a final image of Jody Escobar before she took off on the flight that ended her life… supposedly.

"See that?" he asked. "She had a pack with her when she boarded the Goshawk."

"What of it, Mr. Richmond?"

"It looks like she was packing for a journey rather than running to forestall a disaster." He looked at Quentin. "I need to see the last available footage of Hector before his departure."

By now, Agent Quentin, too, was becoming tired. He pulled the footage. Most of the shots were of Hector speaking to Dr. Gage's new head pilot and Dr. Gage himself.

Watching the two of them was easier for Sam than the stabbing pains footage of Hector and Tamara together caused, but it was still difficult for him to watch Hector interact with the Director as if he had been born to the role. Everyone had loved Hector. That was, until he left.

Disgusted from the unfair and largely unimportant comparison, Sam shifted his attention to Midgard's sparkling dome in the background of the last picture of Hector. It reflected what Sam thought was the burning light of the evening sun, but something about it was off.

"Did anything happen the night before Hector's disappearance was discovered?" he asked.

Quentin waited for a response from the General during a brief hiatus. "Yes, well, sort of," he responded. "There was a huge firestorm west of Midgard's restricted area that day. Ramirez took the Director out to get a better look—that last picture is from right after their return to base."

"It was an artificial firestorm," Sam commented.

Silence. Then Quentin said, "We aren't certain."

"Or you made a bad assumption about that fire," Sam retorted. "I'd bet my life that it was the result of a storm generator, and its purpose was to provide cover for Hector's departure."

Static blared so loudly in his ear that Quentin flinched. "Perhaps," he said. "We know all about that theory of attacks preceding disappearances. But the Midgard Stingray attack remains a considerable outlier."

"Ah, but someone did disappear after the Midgard attack," Sam said affirmatively.

"Whom?" Quentin asked without waiting for guidance.

"Jody Escobar."

Another pause. "Jody Escobar is dead," Quentin said slowly. "The battery explosion incinerated her, but we found her DNA at the crash site."

"Are you sure? Because I am not. I suggest you review those DNA traces. My guess is that they are synthetic or from dead cells, not live ones. If I'm right, you'll be able to reclassify her as missing instead of deceased."

"One moment, Richmond," Quentin said and exited the room. Marlow's eyes were like slits as she observed Sam in the semi-darkness, and they reminded Sam of a snake he had once seen at a reptile reserve. *I wonder what she sounds like,* he wondered. But before he could prompt her to speak, Quentin returned.

"What did you see in that picture of Hector Ramirez in the clinic?" Quentin asked.

Sam felt the perspiration on his hands go from warm to cold. *He knows. He knows I saw something there.* "I—I saw a wound on his head," Sam faltered.

For the first time in the interview, Agent Quentin smiled. "You're not being completely open with us, Mr. Richmond." Sam knew the real source of that observation, though. Before he had time to respond, the Table's surface went hot, and Sam braced himself for the coming onslaught.

The pain was exquisite—so much so that, in the first few seconds, Sam's body did not register its full might, and he only felt heat. Gradually, that heat turned to flame, and he felt as if someone was tearing at his flesh with a razor full of little biting creatures. Unable to control his body's response to this treatment, he heard himself scream and scream again until black and white dots danced before his eyes in between the flashes of red.

The sound of static-cloaked shouts coming from Agent Quentin's earpiece was unmistakable now, and Quentin winced at the volume. Before he could respond, however, the door to the room slammed open and Dr. Stephan Gage burst into the room, closely followed by his brother.

"Stop it!" Sam heard his mentor's voice dimly through the whir of the table's highest setting. His back arched with the rash of pain, and he screamed again.

"Stop it immediately."

After one fearful look at the General, Marlow complied, and Sam's body fell back, quivering, onto the Table's surface.

"Sam!" Dr. Gage held him by the shoulders. "Sam, I'm so sorry. If I had known, I would have been here, and I would have—"

But the threads of Sam's consciousness unraveled before he could learn how his most important supporter had failed to protect him.

CHAPTER TWENTY-FOUR:

THE REVELATION

"Hello, my dear. It's wonderful to see you." Dr. Gage embraced Rowen warmly and then held her at arm's length to better appreciate her beauty. Every time he saw his gorgeous, brilliant daughter, he experienced awe—awe that such a marvelous creature belonged to him.

This time, however, concern marred his joy, and he frowned. "You're thinner since the last time I saw you. Don't they feed you rations appropriate to your rank in the British Isles?"

"Of course, Father," Rowen said lightly. "They wouldn't dare do otherwise. I've been working overtime. That's all." She sat gracefully in a chair and then mirrored his frown. "I'm more worried about you. What is the emergency?"

"Ah, yes," Dr. Gage sighed as he sank into his own chair. "I appreciate your prompt response to my summons. I have a bit of a predicament." He hesitated and then leaned back in his chair. "It's Sam."

"Oh? How is he?"

He looked away. "Brilliant as always and still a consummate professional. Turns out he was right about Ms. Escobar. We've recategorized her as Disappeared. And his tip led us to hunt a stealth satellite or satellites."

"Speaking of which," Rowen interjected, "I delivered your private demarches to our counterparts in Canada and the British Isles as well as some of our other... friends. They've put their space forces on high alert and are seeking any international connections that might be working withthis Banshee person, whoever he is."

Dr. Gage pressed his lips together in a thin, straight line. "Then at least some good may yet come out of this debacle." He stood up and paced, a sign Rowen knew meant that he was agitated. "If I had known Anton was going to Table Sam, I would have—"

"Wait.Uncle Anton Tabled Sam Richmond?" Before her father could catch the look of startled surprise on her face, she replaced it with the neutral mask of a seasoned diplomat.

In contrast, her father's visage was a thundercloud. "Yes. Once again, he overstepped. He's starting to get out of hand."

Rowen's clear green eyes clouded, but she shrugged dismissively. "I don't doubt. It is his nature to push boundaries, even with the people he loves."

"You mean all two of them?"

"Yes," she responded, "even with us." She rose from her seat and put her hand on her father's arm. "I know how you feel about Sam, both as your star pupil and as Miranda Richmond's son. But you must appreciate Uncle Anton's caution in this case. He wants to protect you, and he'll do whatever he feels is necessary to shield you from interference."

"That may be true, but his behavior is frustrating as hell sometimes and, in this case, it was damned counterproductive. In one single, unnecessary stroke, Anton has put all of my plans in jeopardy." He removed Rowen's hand and paced again for a few minutes while she watched him. Then he sighed. "Sam no longer trusts me. He's hiding something now, even if he wasn't before."

She raised her eyebrows. "That's hardly surprising given the circumstances. You knew that was always a possibility."

"Yes, but I chose to ignore the prospective consequences, and now I'm paying for it. Argh," he groaned and threw up his hands, "We will all pay unless I can get Sam back in our corner."

The sound of stifled mirth made him turn around to stare at his daughter. "Do you mind telling me what you find so amusing about this fiasco?"

"Actually, nothing about this situation is funny." Rowen grinned. "But I just figured out why you wanted me here and, yes, I think I can help."

* * *

Sam lay on his back and stared at the ceiling of his old room at Midgard. A throbbing pain behind his eyes threatened to blossom into a full-blown migraine, and his skin crawled with the memories of its recent ordeal at the Table's hands. A wave of nausea surfaced and crested within his stomach. Abruptly, he sat up and snatched a container he had stowed under his pillow.

With shaking hands, he removed its lid and tossed two dissolvable pills into his mouth. A cold sweat broke across his forehead as he dry-heaved with the effort of keeping them down. After a minute or so, numbness crept outward from his stomach to his head, and he breathed a sigh of relief. The pain was gone, but its sudden absence left him too drained to do anything but return to his bunk.

He had repeated this routine every afternoon since his return Midgard. A horrified Stephan Gage had rescued him—albeit too late—from the General's clutches at the Utengard headquarters and spirited him back under his protection. Sam spent nearly a week in the clinic undergoing specialized counter-Table therapies before returning to part-time duty working on his special task. His mornings were spent doing research in Dr. Gage's office, and at his physician's insistence, his afternoons consisted of more therapy followed by a few hours of recovery time.

Even with an unprecedented amount of rest, Sam felt blown, both physically and mentally, and he felt as if he existed somewhere on a plane between agony and detachment.

"How long will I be like this?" he had asked Dr. Malika earlier in the day.

"I'm not sure," she responded. "My guess would be a month or so, but it's hard to say. That amount of system shock is dangerous and—"

A doorbell chime interrupted these those thoughts, and Sam's eyes snapped open. *That's odd.* Dr. Gage had posted guards outside his door to prevent anyone from interrupting his recovery time.

"Enter," he said and sat up. The door slid open and revealed a petite young woman with the remnants of what had once been a head full of lively, dark curls.

"Tam," he breathed, his voice and senses dulled by the medicine. He moved toward the ladder at the edge of his bunk but stopped when she raised her hand.

"Don't get up! I know you're not… well. Let me come to you."

Dizzy with both surprise and the aftereffects of the medication, he nodded and reclined against his pillow. She climbed the ladder and sat at Sam's feet, much as she used to do when they were children. But she had changed so much since he had last seen her that he barely recognized her. Tamara had lost her pudginess and was almost gaunt. Faint burn scars crept up her neck as if the flames that caused them had welded into her skin. Enormous black smudges shadowed hereyes, which, though still large and beautiful, no longer glowed with their trademark warmth and light. Instead, they were dull, as if someone had thrown mud in a tidepool.

"How are you, Tam?" he asked.

She rolled her eyes in a shadow of her former self. "How am I, Sam?" she asked, sarcastically."Geez. Let me see. In the last two months, my transport was shot out of the sky, and I barely escaped with my life, my fiancé joined the ranks of the Disappeared, I spent a week being interrogated, and my—" she looked sidelong at Sam, "best friend, who hasn't spoken to me since I turned him down, got Tabled. Other than that, I'm doing just dandy, thank you."

The exhaustion behind the sarcasm mirrored his own weariness, which went far beyond the physical, and his first impulse was to console her. "If it makes you feel any better, I don't think Hector intended to leave you behind."

She froze. "What? What are you talking about?"

Sam exhaled and held out his arm. "Can you help me up, please? I want to show you something."

Seeing his pallor, Tamara bit back the barrage of questions she wanted to bombard him with. Slowly, she guided him out of bed and down the ladder, ready to brace him if he fell.

The touch of her hands sent a jolt through him, and her grip tightened.

"Are you dizzy?" she asked.

"No... I... Tam... I—" he stammered, and then bent over and touched her hair with his lips. She was so warm, and the familiar scents of fresh soil and earth that emanated from her body were intoxicating. It—she—was the one thing in his life that had remained true, and he moved his lips downward to hers.

At first, she stiffened. Then her lips parted automatically at the urgent pressure from his own.

The kiss started slowly and gained momentum as Sam savored her smell, her taste, and the odd but pleasant feel of her shortened hair. It was wonderful, the most wonderful feeling in the world, and in that moment, it blotted out everything else. He felt alive, really and truly alive for the first time he could remember and—

And then he realized that Tamara had gone rigid in his arms.

"Sam, stop. Please stop." She pressed back on his shoulders and held him apart. Tears streamed down her cheeks, but she was resolute. "We can't do this."

Stop. Please stop. They were the same words she had used to reject him in the clinic. The blow stunned him. He stepped back, felt blindly for the chair to his desk, and stumbled into it.

"You're still in love with him. Aren't you?"

She sat on the one remaining chair in the room and nodded. "Yeah."

He pressed his hands to his eyes. "I'm so sorry, Tam. It's just that... I didn't mean—" *I didn't want it to be this way,* was what he wanted to say, but the cliché sounded hollow.

"I wish—" She faltered. He looked up, and she saw that the haunted look had returned.

"Tam?"

"I wish we could... Well, I wish we could befriends again. I know it won't be the same as before, but..." She looked at Sam's troubled countenance. "I should go," she whispered and stood up to leave.

"No. Wait. I need to show you something. Something important."

She eyed him warily. "What is it? Have you found—" She stopped when she saw him press a finger to his lips and look meaningfully toward the guarded door. He opened the top drawer to his desk and pulled out a thin metal stylus. Before she could ask what it was, he pressed it to his upper right arm, and its tip glowed white.

"There," he said. "We have about ten minutes before the effects of my interceptor wear off."

Her eyes were wide. "What on earth—"

"I don't have time to explain all of that," he said impatiently, "but I need to talk to you without being monitored. And you cannot relay this information to anyone. It will put us both at risk, but you especially.Okay?"

"Okay."

He palmed into the terminal and spent the next minute tunneling through Midgard's security protocols.Once his countersurveillance program finished, he pulled up a cache of images and trawled through them, his fingers moving at lightning speed. Eventually, he stopped, and four pictures remained on his display.

"Come. Look at this," he said.

Befuddled, Tamara leaned over his shoulder.

"What do you see?"

"I see four left hands," she responded, puzzled.

"Look closer." He pointed to the screen.

"Um, they all have freckles?"

"Yes, they do, but look at the pattern."

"I don't see a pattern."

"Right. Let me show you." He tapped the screen and three of the four hands rotated until all of the freckles aligned in the same shape.

Tamara's jaw dropped. "Which constellation is that?" she asked.

"It isn't a constellation.Now, watch while I adjust the light filter on these pictures." He manipulated the display, and the hand images gradually turned color from white to orange to red. After a few seconds, a faint glimmer appeared and connected the freckles on the hands.

Sam stopped the simulation. "Exactly 911 nanometers," he triumphed.

"Wait," Tamara cried. "I've seen that symbol before. It's—"

"It's the same as this," Sam said and pulled Miranda's pendant from inside his uniform.

Tamara reached for the silver disc as if she was in a trance and held it in her shaking palm."Yes," she breathed as she studied the symbol. "Whose hands are they?"

"Jody Escobar's, Hector Delacroix's, my mother's, and Hector's, all from between one and three months before they disappeared."

"How did you make the connection?"

Sam smiled wryly at Tamara's unintentional play on words. "I caught a glimpse of something on Jody's hand during one of our training runs, and I saw something odd on Hector's hand in the clinic." He held out his own hand and pointed. "Hector and I have a similar skin tone, and neither of us freckles. But I mistook those marks on his hand for dirt or burns or burn marks at the time."

Sam hesitated before he made his next admission. "I also saw the spiral on my own hand, but it was only in a dream."

"A dream?" Tamara asked, confused.

"Yes, I've been having dreams that are too vivid and consequential to be coincidence." His face darkened. "Anyhow, I confirmed my theory about these light tattoos during my—encounter—with the Table, but I chose not to disclose those findings to my inquisitors and—" he shrugged and gestured to his wasted frame, "you now see the results."

"Oh, Sam, you should have just told them and—"

"And potentially put Hector's life in danger? Or my mother's? Hell no. They left for a reason, Tam, and I will get to the bottom of it or die trying." He turned his attention back to his terminal. "And I've made some progress already." He gave his system a series of commands so complex that its screen burned with the energy required to absorb and compute the details. When he was finished, Tamara saw map of the United States with four bright dots on it.

"These show the locations of where each of them disappeared," Sam explained and tapped in some additional instructions. The number of dots increased in clusters until the entire map was illuminated.

"All of those people have disappeared?" Tamara asked, awed. "But there must be thousands—tens of thousands of them. Far greater numbers than anyone knows about."

"That's because our government only tracks those who came from high-Tier positions. They discount others, including indigents and vagrants and," he added as an afterthought, "terrorists, rebels, and dissidents." He pointed to the screen. "These people came from all kinds of professions and backgrounds. They were scientists, technologists, and engineers, but at least half of them were creators—artists and writers and actors and musicians—capabilities no longer valued in our dying world."

He gave Tamara a moment to absorb the information and then held her eyes with an intensity reminiscent of his old self. "Whoever is collecting these people isn't trying to overthrow a government or take over the Capsule Program or weaponize a virus or anything like that.They're building a new society—a colony."

She inhaled sharply. "What do you mean weaponize a virus?"

Sam's head began to throb again as did his right arm. "I don't have time to get into that now," he said wearily. "But just know that I've lost faith in Midgard and the Capsule program, Tam, and I'm looking for an escape route." He looked up at her. "And when I find it, I'm taking you with me. I promise."

She sat and stared at him numbly before she shook her head. "I can't leave my father behind, Sam."

He shook his head. "You don't need to. He disappeared three days ago.The colony—whoever they are—must have needed a sculptor or architect."

"What!" she screeched and jumped to her feet. Sam reached and put his hand over her mouth as he glanced nervously at the door. When guards did not burst through it, he removed his hand and again pressed his finger to his lips.

"How could he, how could he go without—without telling me?" She began to sob.

Sam patted her on the back awkwardly. "It's a good sign, actually. No one who disappears ever tells anyone they're leaving. It must be one of the colony's rules. They get that light tattoo on their hand, and they're gone within weeks. That is the only clue." He waited for her to stop crying. "The clips I pulled indicate that your father got his sometime last month."

Tamara sniffled and wiped her eyes. "You said something about Hector not wanting to leave me behind before we—"

Sam slumped. "Right. Well, I can't prove it yet, but I think Hector was supposed to be evacuated by the paramilitary forces that shot you down, but they miscalculated the trajectory of their missiles. A secret facility was in the way. Anyhow, instead of forcing a landing, they almost destroyed the Stingray instead, and Hector had no choice but to leave you at Midgard after you were injured."

Tamara digested this news in silence. "So, you think you can find out where he—where all of those people went? That's going to be hard given that no one else has been able to do that. Unless you have another dream about where—"

She stopped when she saw him shake his head. "I haven't had any dreams like that since the Table," he said flatly. He did not add that those telling dreams had been replaced by nightmares in which various creatures—and people—flayed him open one skin cell at a time.

"So, how are you going to find the colony?"

Sam smiled grimly. "The General gave me a clue."

"General who?" she asked, baffled.

"That's not important," he said irritably. "What is important is that his slip connected nicely with an image from the last dream I had." He returned to the terminal and pulled up a picture of a middle-aged man with black and white hair in a braid on one side of his head. He had a star-shaped scar on his left cheek.

"Who is that?"

"That," Sam said with alacrity, "is the leader of the organization behind all of the diversions that precede high-profile disappearances. His name is Ansel Merek, but his codename from his time in the service was Banshee."

She shook her head and rolled her eyes. "How are you going to find someone whose alias means 'ghost,' Sam?

Sam grinned at her. "I'm not going to find him, Tam. My intention is to get him to come to me."

End of Book 1

ACKNOWLEDGMENTS

The most rewarding thing about writing *Midgard,* my first novel, was not the writing itself, which surprised me. It was the sheer volume of support from family and friends, many of whom I had lost touch with. Getting back in contact with many of them was the highlight of this undertaking, and I owe every one of them my gratitude.

First, I am grateful to my husband, Scott, and my son Gabriel for not giving me grief when I devoted nights and weekends to writing classes and writing instead of spending quality time with them. Scott also served as my tactical advisor, and his assessments of future warfare helped enliven some of my action scenes.

I also had a battalion of invisible supporters—those who influenced me to listen to my intuition and let the long-repressed author out of her oubliette. Some of them are mentioned in my dedication, but many, many others I hope are content with thoughts of thanks. In addition, I will mention a handful here, starting with my cousin, Kelly Sener. She really got the wheels turning when she took me to the Strand Bookstore in New York City. There I visualized signing my own book for readers for the very first time. My hypnotherapist, Margie Majors, reinforced this vision, and my Clarity on Fire coach, Rachel East, helped me reestablish a relationship with my inner child and her desire to create. Rachel's business partner, Kristen Walker, later informed me that she was in the process of writing a book, and she introduced me to the inestimable Eric Koester, founder of the Creator Institute.

Eric Koester's energy and enthusiasm for helping people like me move from idea to manuscript to actual book is both contagious and boundless, and he and his fellow professor Hailey Newlin motivated me to see the process through. My developmental editor, Tom Toner, assisted me with the transition from academic writer to storyteller through his candid feedback, dry humor, and upbeat approach. Alan Zatkow, my master revisions editor at New Degree Press, worked vigorously to help refine those skills, and he taught me the different muscles of writing—and how and when to flex them—in the process. The rest of the editors, writers, and publishing staff at New Degree Press did a superb job polishing my rough gemstone and turning it into a quality story.

Finally, my manuscript would have been stuck collecting dust in cyberspace were it not for the financial and emotional support from my sponsors and my author community. My wonderful employers at IT Cadre, Mark Madigan and Mike Morrisroe, were so enthusiastic about my endeavor that they decided to get a copy of the book for every member of the company. I was also blown away by support from my family and friends, including my parents and siblings, my husband's family and siblings, my fellow USMA and Princeton alumnus, veterans, and colleagues. In no particular order, they are: Steve and Marian Hull, John and Linda Sener, Tim and Sara Hull, Greg Hull, Geoff Hull, Christopher and Lauren Godfroy, Nancy Moss, Kathy Letourneau, John and Sandy Bengston, Steve and Jamie Minihane,

Steve Kuo, Rudy and Helene Sheahan, Madeline Ferrucci, Robert Branchaud, Lucas and Sarah Dorosky, Steve and Shayne Johnson, Tom and Julie Cooper, Dave and Carolyn Nash, Eric and Shannon Duckworth, Liz and John McNally, Greg Ferrando, Gene and Jess Szatkowski, Doug Mercado, Adam Keith, Andy and Hartleigh Caine, Casey Martinez, Mary Link, Kim Compton, Mike Kopicko, Mike Tilton, Jimmy "Demo" Demonstranti, Nancy McBride, Randy Overstreet, Ed Cox, Irv Oliver, Aaron Willis, Kyle Gentle, Jennifer Walker, David Escobar, Josh and Karen Mendoza, Catherine Miller, Jen Welsh, Jason and Samantha Galui, Noah Segal, Rob Sweetman, Elsa Bullard, Svea Thunhorst, Connor Matteson, Susanne Varga, and Brian Scott. Thank you all so much for helping me finance publication and for providing me with valuable feedback and encouragement in response to my incessant emails, surveys, Linkedin postings, and Instagram messages.

If it takes a proverbial village to raise a child, it takes at least a hamlet to bring a first novel to fruition, or so I've discovered. I am eternally grateful to the members of Midgard's hamlet for helping me turn my dream into reality.

Made in United States
North Haven, CT
05 September 2024

57029888R00143